WAR ON LAND

THE BRITANNICA GUIDE TO WAR

WAR ON LAND

EDITED BY ROBERT CURLEY, MANAGER, SCIENCE AND TECHNOLOGY

Britannica®
Educational Publishing

IN ASSOCIATION WITH

ROSEN
EDUCATIONAL SERVICES

Published in 2012 by Britannica Educational Publishing
(a trademark of Encyclopædia Britannica, Inc.)
in association with Rosen Educational Services, LLC
29 East 21st Street, New York, NY 10010.

Distributed exclusively by Rosen Educational Services.
For a listing of additional Britannica Educational Publishing titles, call toll free (800) 237-9932.

First Edition

Britannica Educational Publishing
Michael I. Levy: Executive Editor
Adam Augustyn: Assistant Manager, Encyclopædia Britannica
Marilyn L. Barton: Senior Coordinator, Production Control
Steven Bosco: Director, Editorial Technologies
Lisa S. Braucher: Senior Producer and Data Editor
Yvette Charboneau: Senior Copy Editor
Robert Curley: Manager, Science and Technology

Rosen Educational Services
Jeanne Nagle: Editor
Nelson Sá: Art Director
Cindy Reiman: Photography Manager
Brian Garvey: Designer
Introduction by Heather Moore Niver

Library of Congress Cataloging-in-Publication Data

War on land/edited by Robert Curley.
    p. cm.—(The Britannica guide to war)
"In association with Britannica Educational Publishing, Rosen Educational Services."
Includes bibliographical references and index.
ISBN 978-1-61530-697-8 (library binding)
1. Military art and science—History. 2. Military history. I. Curley, Robert, 1955–
U27.W342 2012
355.4—dc23

2011035887

Manufactured in the United States of America

On the cover: U.S. soldiers on foot patrol in western Baghdad, Iraq, in November 2005.
David Furst/AFP/Getty Images

On pp. 1, 22, 40, 55, 71, 91, 102, 120, 143, 162: U.S. Marines disembarking an amphibious
assault vehicle during training exercises in Hawaii, 2004. *Jane West/U.S. Navy photo
(040718-N-5055W-066)*

CONTENTS

Introduction   x

**CHAPTER 1: PREHISTORIC AND
EARLY WARFARE**   1

The Earliest Military Weapons   2
From Precious Metals to Base Metals   4
Antiquity and the Classical Age   5
   The Phalanx and the Legion   5
   Military Technology of the Period   7
   Defensive Weaponry   8
   Types of Armour   11
   Offensive Weaponry   12
   Arrows   16
   Mechanical Artillery   17
   Fortification   18
   Land Transportation   19

CHAPTER 2: WAR IN THE MIDDLE AGES   22

The Age of Cavalry   22
   The Medieval Knight   23
   The War-Horse   27
   The Castle   29
Siege Weapons   31
   The Trebuchet   31
   Greek Fire   32
The Horse Archer   33
   The Huns and Avars   33
   The Byzantine Cataphract   33
   The Turks   34
   The Mongols   34
The Infantry Revolution   35
   The Crossbow   36
   The English Longbow   38
   Halberd and Pike   39

**CHAPTER 3: THE GUNPOWDER
REVOLUTION**   40

Early Gunpowder   42
   Serpentine Powder   42
   Corned Powder   42
   Gunpowder Recipes   43
   Refinements in Ballistics   44

9

37

The Development of Artillery   45
    Wrought-Iron Muzzle-Loaders   45
    Wrought-Iron Breechloaders   46
    Cast Bronze Muzzle-Loaders   48
    Cast-Iron Cannons   49
Early Use of Artillery   50
    Special-Purpose Shot   51
    Gunnery   52
    The First Small Arms   52
    The Matchlock   52
    The Wheel Lock   53
    The Flintlock   53

CHAPTER 4: FORTIFICATION AND MODERN BODY ARMOUR   55

Fortification   56
    The Effect of Artillery and Siegecraft on
    Fortification Design   56
    The Sunken Profile   57
    The Bastioned Trace   59
    Duration of Early Modern Fortification 59
Trench Warfare, 1850–1918   60
    The Siege of Petersburg   61
Permanent Fortification During World War I 62
The Maginot Line and the West Wall
in World War II   62
    Other Fort Series   63
German Channel Defenses in World War II   63
Nuclear Fortification   64
Body Armour   65
    New Materials   67
    Modern Body Armour Systems   68

CHAPTER 5: MODERN SMALL ARMS: SHOULDER WEAPONS AND PISTOLS   71

Shoulder Weapons   71
    Smoothbore Muzzle-Loaders   72
    Rifled Muzzle-Loaders   75
    Breechloaders   77
    The Many Uses of Guncotton   80
    Automatic Weapons   82
    The Assault Rifle   85

Pistols 88
   Revolvers 88
   Samuel Colt 89
   Self-Loaders 89

Chapter 6: Machine Guns and Specialty Shoulder Weapons   91

Early Manual Multibarreled Weapons 91
   The Gatling Gun 91
   Richard J. Gatling 92
   The Mitrailleuse 92
Heavy Machine Guns 93
   Recoil 93
   Gas Operation 94
   Blowback 94
Light Machine Guns 95
Large-Calibre Machine Guns 96
Grenade Launchers 97
   Single Shot 97
   Automatic Fire 98
Antitank Weapons 100

Chapter 7: Modern Artillery   102

Cannons 102
   Rifled Bores 103
   Recoil Control 106
   Carriages and Mountings 107
   Big Bertha 109
   Fire Control 110
   Ammunition 112
Mortars 115
Antiaircraft Artillery 115
   Heavy Weapons and the Problem
   of Fire Control 116
   Light Weapons 116
Antitank Guns 118
Recoilless Guns 119

Chapter 8: Tanks and Other Armoured Vehicles   120

Tanks 120
   Earliest Developments 120

World War I   121
Interwar Developments   123
World War II   125
The Sherman Tank   126
Postwar Tank Development   128
Other Armoured Vehicles   134
Armoured Personnel Carriers   134
Amphibious Assault Vehicles   136
Infantry Fighting Vehicles   137
Wheeled Armoured Vehicles   139

**CHAPTER 9: ROCKET AND
MISSILE SYSTEMS**   **143**
Military Rockets   143
The Congreve Rocket   144
*Francis Scott Key and the Star
Spangled Banner*   146
Rocketry Research and
Experimentation   147
Barrage Rockets   149
Bazookas and Panzerschrecks   150
Antiaircraft Rockets and Aerial
Rockets in World War II   152
Tactical Guided Missiles   153
Guidance Methods   153
Guided-Missile Systems   155

CONCLUSION   **162**

Glossary   163
Bibliography   165
Index   169

128

139

151

INTRODUCTION

As long as humans have roamed the Earth, there has been war. History books are voluminous with tales of conflict through the ages. Wars have taken place in many different geographic areas—also called theatres or military ecospheres—and have been waged in the air, at sea, and on the ground. This volume examines conflicts as they occur in the last arena, with a focus on the weaponry, fortifications, and personal protection used through the ages by warriors on land. From the walls of Jericho to computer-driven missiles of the 21st century, readers will be able to trace the gradual advancement of military tactics and technologies.

In prehistoric times, military might was dictated largely by what the human body could (and could not) do. Geography and topography were mitigating factors as well. The first tool specifically designed as a weapon was the mace, a rock shaped to fit the hand that was used for smashing bone and flesh. Later, a handle was added for extra power. Primitive humans discovered that early hunting tools made of wood and stone, such as the spear and the bow and arrow, also made effective weapons.

Metal succeeded stone as the material of choice for weaponry as early as the 2nd and 3rd millennia BCE. Precious metals such as gold and silver were, at first, heavily favoured because they were so easily moulded into helmets and body armour. Base metals weren't as malleable, but they were stronger and more effective. Precious metals were replaced by copper, which was superseded by bronze implements. Iron weapons, including axes, spears, and swords, were developed during late antiquity and were used until the fall of Rome. Shields, helmets, and mail were among the early forms of military defensive, or protective, items made first of bronze, then of iron.

Horses, elephants, and chariots (which were pulled by draft animals such as horses) were used in battle to some degree, but issues of strength, mobility, and economic viability greatly curtailed their involvement in ancient warfare. For the most part, soldiers traveled by and fought on foot through the classical age. Ranks made up of several lines of heavily armed men charged into battle shoulder to shoulder in a Greek-developed formation called the phalanx. This formation is thought to be the kernel of European military development.

As with most political, social, economic, and cultural structures of society, the waging of war also underwent significant change during the Middle Ages. Warriors on horseback dated as far back as the 1st century CE, with the

An engraving depicting a battle between French and English forces during the Hundred Years' War. Kean Collection/Archive Photos/Getty Images nomadic horse archer. In 378 CE, Gothic horsemen defeated Roman legions at the Battle of Adrianople, ushering in the age of cavalry in Europe. Skilled riders rode specially bred steeds that were strong and fast. In the Middle Ages, professional cavalrymen were known as knights. On the battlefield, knights wore mail tunics and plate armour and were opposed by foot soldiers who wielded weapons such as crossbows and longbows. The taking of fortresses and castles required heavier weapons. Large battering rams could break through doors and gates, trebuchets could hurl heavy objects like rocks against castle walls, and Greek fire—a mysterious, flammable liquid that could not be extinguished by water—was pumped or hurled onto enemy troops.

Weaponry, and warfare, entered a new era once gunpowder entered the equation. Up until this time, weapons were powered by human muscle alone. Gunpowder freed weapon design to focus on tactical demands. The Chinese developed the earliest gunpowder, which today is called black powder—a mixture of potassium nitrate (or saltpetre) charcoal, and sulfur—in the 9th century CE. Four centuries later, Europeans adopted black powder as a propellant and explosive.

The means by which weapons-grade gunpowder was produced and refined evolved over the centuries. Initially, the dry ingredients were ground separately and then mixed together to make what was called serpentine. After 1400, the dry ingredients were ground together with water, creating a slurry that was then dried into sheets or cakes. Further processing rendered it into pieces as large as a grain of corn, thus giving it the name corned powder. Larger-grained powder was best for cannons while medium grains were destined for use in shoulder arms such as muskets; the fine powder left behind during processing was used in smaller guns such as pistols.

The earliest guns were likely made of brass or bronze, but wrought iron was cheaper and withstood extreme temperatures. Smiths forged wrought-ion muzzleloaders and breechloaders and also used cast bronze for single pieces that were large and asymmetrical. At first handguns were basically "hand cannons"—designed and operated much like cannons on a smaller scale—that required two people to fire. Then, starting in the 15th century, small firearms became a class of weapon all their own. The matchlock gave way to the wheel lock, which, in turn, led to the development of the flintlock.

The cast-iron cannon was quite heavy compared to its bronze counterpart and tended to corrode from within, but its low production cost made it popular. Frequently artillery troops took a one-two approach when using cannons to lay siege to a castle or other fortification. Cannonballs of iron were fired at the bottom of a fortress wall, weakening the foundation, and then the rest of the wall was obliterated by a barrage of heavy stone shot. In response, the design of fortifications changed. Fortress walls were sunk into the ground, polygonal bastions were added, and walls and towers were reinforced.

Castles were permanent defenses. Temporary, or field, fortifications came into popular use in the United States during the American Civil War, when troops secured a newly won position by literally "digging in." Soldiers drew spades and axes from their packs and dug rifle pits that were expanded into long trenches. Both Confederate and Union soldiers engaged the enemy in firefights from the relative safety of trenches.

European troops incorporated trench warfare during World War I, adding sandbags and barbed wire to their earthy fortifications. After the war, great concrete forts were built with tremendous walls and elaborate artillery pieces, essentially serving as outposts to protect long stretches of coastline or inland territory. Fortress complexes such as France's Maginot Line constituted the modern military's answer to castles and other ancient permanent fortifications. Following World War II, the threat of nuclear attack prompted several nations to build reinforced concrete bunkers beneath the earth's surface, thus taking permanent fortifications underground.

In the 20th century, there was a return of gear designed to protect soldiers personally—lighter, more adaptable versions of a medieval warrior's armour. During World War I, helmets were worn to protect the skull from bullets whizzing past the head and shrapnel from artillery barrages. Armoured, or "bullet-proof," vests were introduced toward the end of the Korean conflict of the 1950s. Since that time revolutionary new materials such as Kevlar have given modern warriors body armour that is lighter and even more protective.

Military small arms have undergone a number of changes since the creation of the flintlock in the 1600s. Experiments with various projectiles and chemical propellants have helped reduce the weight of such guns without limiting their deadliness. Smoothbore muzzle loaders took advantage of the flintlock ignition system, but they were still quite heavy and they were difficult to aim with any degree of accuracy beyond 75 yards. Gun barrels with spiral grooves carved into them were said to be "rifled," giving a new type of shoulder weapon its name. Early muzzle-loading rifles were initially slow to load, but inventors overcame this problem by developing projectiles such as the Minié ball, which could be easily dropped down the barrel, was not deformed while loading, and expanded on firing to fit the rifled grooves so that accuracy improved. Breechloaders, rifles that were loaded with ammunition from the back, or base of the barrel, saw a lot of action in the American Civil War, but these early guns were apt to misfire and tended to leak gas and flame. Breechloaders were not practical or reliable until the invention of the cartridge, which sealed both bullet and gunpowder in a single case. Cartridges led to the development of bolt-action rifles, which transformed the battlefield toward the end of the 19th century.

The next incarnation of military shoulder arms was the self-loading rifle, which did not go into heavy production until after World War I. Semiautomatic weapons, which use energy or gas created when a round is fired to remove the used cartridge case, fire only one shot with each trigger pull. Assault rifles and submachine guns are fully automatic, firing as long as there is ammunition loaded and the trigger is depressed. Assault rifles, such as the AK-47, can switch from semiautomatic to fully automatic.

Soldiers have toted pistols into battle since the 16th century, but only the most skilled soldiers could get an accurate shot at any distance. Most troops used revolvers and similar automatic pistols as auxiliary weapons to their shoulder arms during World War II. Today, pistols are primarily sidearms for military police personnel.

Multibarreled weapons such as the Gatling gun and the mitrailleuse saw limited military use—by U.S. and French troops, respectively—in the late 19th century. The search for increased firepower continued, eventually leading to the development of larger, infantry-support weapons such as machine guns and grenade launchers.

Self-actuated heavy machine guns wrought havoc during conflicts in the later years of the 19th century and during World War I. Because of their heft, these were more effective as defensive, rather than offensive, weapons. In the 1930s, a number of lighter machine guns, sometimes referred to as automatic rifles, were manufactured by several countries for military use.

Grenades were popular weapons in the modern era but their range was limited to how far a soldier could throw them. Enter the grenade launcher, a weapon whose sole purpose was to propel grenades farther with great accuracy. Shoulder-fired launchers were used for single-shot grenades. These weapons also have been mounted on tripods, armoured vehicles, and helicopters. Similar in construction and application were antitank weapons such as the bazooka.

Tanks themselves became an integral military weapon, beginning in earnest with the dawn of the 20th century. Basically, tanks are tracked fighting vehicles incorporating everything from rifle-calibre machine guns to large-bore, long-barrelled guns. Thick, resistant armour protects the crews inside. Joining tanks in the ranks of tracked military vehicles are armoured personnel carriers, infantry fighting vehicles, and amphibious assault vehicles, the latter capable of transporting troops over both water and land. Wheeled armoured vehicles attend to many tasks, including infantry transport, scouting and exploration, antitank defense, fire support, and medical evacuation, to name a few.

Some armoured vehicles have been adapted to carry rocket launchers. Rockets are explosive or incendiary weapons that are propelled toward a target at great distance. Military rockets are thought to have originated in 1232, when Chinese troops rained fiery "arrows" (which were accompanied by a thunderous explosion) upon Mongol invaders. Early rockets were a crude affair, essentially paper-and-shellac tubes stuffed with gunpowder. By 1668 engineers in Germany had developed a rocket made of wood and sailcloth that was capable of carrying a larger, more potent load of explosive material. Rocket use dwindled over the course of the next century but experienced a resurgence in the 18th century, when metal cylinders were used to contain the explosive powder. From there, various advances and improvements were made to rocketry weapons through the years, including the addition of powerful engines and fins that extended a rocket's range and increased its accuracy.

Guided missiles have greatly superseded traditional unguided rockets as a military weapon. Missiles have the same deadly explosive capabilities of rockets, but their advantage is that they can be guided toward a specific target with astounding accuracy.

War has inspired everything from patriotism and awe to horror and disgust, and understandably so. It is a sociopolitical phenomenon that is destined to arise as long as citizens are willing to fight for advantage or to die for what they believe is a just cause. Aiding and abetting participants in these armed conflicts are technological advances that, over time, have made all human endeavours (including inflicting pain on fellow human beings) more efficient and effective. As preferable as it would be to live in an age of peace, war—and the accompanying technology that makes modern warfare possible—seems to be part of a daunting reality we all must face for the foreseeable future.

CHAPTER 1

PREHISTORIC AND EARLY WARFARE

In the remote past, the diffusion of military technology was gradual and uneven. There were several reasons for this. First, transport was slow and its capacity small. Second, the technology of agriculture was no more advanced than that of war, so that, with most of their energy devoted to feeding themselves and with little economic surplus, people had few resources available for specialized military technology. Low economic development meant that even the benefits of conquest would not pay off a heavy investment in weaponry. Third, and most important, the absolute level of technological development was low. A heavy dependence on human muscle was the principal cause and a major effect of this low level of development. With human ingenuity bound by the constraints of the human body, both technology and tactics were heavily shaped by geography, climate, and topography.

The importance of geographic and topographic factors, along with limited means of communication and transportation, meant that separate geographic regions tended to develop unique military technologies. Such areas are called military ecospheres. The boundaries of a military ecosphere might be physical barriers, such as oceans or mountain ranges; they might also be changes in the military topography, that combination of terrain, vegetation, and man-made features that could render a particular technology or tactic effective or ineffective.

Until the late 15th century CE, when advances in transportation technology broke down the barriers between them, the world contained a number of military eco-spheres. The most clearly defined of these were based in Mesoamerica, Japan, India–Southeast Asia, China, and Europe. (In this context, Europe includes all of the Mediterranean basin and the watershed of the Tigris and Euphrates rivers.) With the appearance of the horse archer in late antiquity, the Eurasian Steppe became a well-defined military ecosphere as well.

Those ecospheres with the most enduring impact on the technology of war were the European and Chinese. Though Japan possessed a distinctive, coher-ent, and effective military technology, it had little influence on developments elsewhere. India–Southeast Asia and Mesoamerica developed technologies that were well adapted to local condi-tions, but they were not particularly advanced. The Eurasian Steppe was a special case. Usually serving as an ave-nue for a limited exchange of knowledge between Europe and China, in the late classical and medieval eras of Europe this ecosphere developed an indigenous mili-tary technology based on the horse and composite recurved bow that challenged Europe and, ultimately, conquered China.

Improved methods of transportation and warfare led to the eventual disap-pearance of the regional ecospheres and their absorption into the European ecosphere. This process began in the 12th century with the Mongol conquest of China and invasions of Europe, and it quickened and assumed a more pro-nounced European flavour in the 15th

and 16th centuries with the development of oceangoing ships armed with gunpow-der weapons.

THE EARLIEST MILITARY WEAPONS

The earliest evidence for a special-ized technology of war dates from the period before knowledge of metalwork-ing had been acquired. The stone walls of Jericho, which date from about 8000 BCE, represent the first technology that can be ascribed unequivocally to purely military purposes. These walls, at least 4 metres (13 feet) in height and backed by a watchtower or redoubt some 8.5 metres (28 feet) tall, were clearly intended to pro-tect the settlement and its water supply from human intruders.

When the defenses of Jericho were built, humans already had been using the weapons of the hunt for mil-lennia; the earliest stone tools are hundreds of thousands of years old, and the first arrowheads date to more than 60,000 years ago. Hunting tools—the spear-thrower (atlatl), the simple bow, the javelin, and the sling—had serious military potential, but the first known implements designed purposely as offen-sive weapons were maces dating from the Chalcolithic Period or early Bronze Age. The mace was a simple rock, shaped for the hand and intended to smash bone and flesh, to which a handle had been added to increase the velocity and force of the blow.

Huns riding into battle in an illustration by A. de Neuville. Two of the men are shown with spiked ball maces. Kean Collection/Archive Photos/Getty Images

It is evident that the technical problems of hafting a stone onto a handle were not easily solved. Well-made maces were for a long time few in number and were, by and large, wielded only by champions and rulers. The earliest known inscription identifying a historical personage by name is on the palette of King Narmer, a small, low-relief slate sculpture dating from about 3100 BCE. The palette depicts Menes, the first pharaoh of a unified Egypt, ritually smashing the forehead of an enemy with a mace.

The advent of the mace as a purposely designed offensive weapon opened the door to the conscious innovation of specialized military technology. By the middle of the 3rd millennium BCE, mace heads were being cast of copper, first in Mesopotamia and then in Syria, Palestine, and Egypt. The copper mace head, yielding higher density and greater crushing power, represents one of the earliest significant uses of metal for other than ornamental purposes.

FROM PRECIOUS METALS TO BASE METALS

The dividing line between the utilitarian and the symbolic in warfare has never been clear and unequivocal, and this line is particularly difficult to find in the design and construction of early weaponry. The engineering principles that dictated functional effectiveness were not understood in any systematic fashion, yet the psychological reality of victory or defeat was starkly evident. The result was an "unscientific" approach to warfare and technology, in which materials appear to have been applied to military purposes as much for their presumed mystical or magical properties as for their functional worth.

This overlapping of symbolism and usefulness is most evident in the smith's choice of materials. Ornaments and ceremonial artifacts aside, metalworking was applied to the production of weaponry as early as, or earlier than, any other economically significant pursuit. Precious metals, with their low melting points and great malleability, were worked first; next came copper—at first pure, then alloyed with arsenic or tin to produce bronze—and then iron. A remarkable phenomenon was the persistence of weaponry made of the soft, rare metals such as gold, silver, and electrum (a naturally occurring alloy of gold and silver) long after mechanically superior materials had become available. Although they were functionally inferior to bronze or copper, precious metals were widely valued for their mystical or symbolic importance, and smiths continued to make weapons of them long after they had mastered the working of functionally superior base metals. Some of these weapons were plainly ceremonial, but in other cases they appear to have been functional. For example, helmets and body armour of electrum, which were probably intended for actual use, have been found in Egyptian and Mesopotamian burials dating from the 2nd and 3rd millennia BCE.

ANTIQUITY AND THE CLASSICAL AGE

From the appearance of iron weaponry in quantity during late antiquity until the fall of Rome, the means with which war was waged and the manner in which it was conducted displayed many enduring characteristics that gave the period surprising unity. Prominent features of that unity were a continuity in the design of individual weaponry, a relative lack of change in transportation technology, and an enduring tactical dominance of heavy infantry.

THE PHALANX AND THE LEGION

From the very earliest times, the preferred tactical formation for sending men into battle consisted of a block of heavily armed infantry standing shoulder to shoulder in files several ranks deep. This formation is known as the

Macedonian troops standing shoulder to shoulder, forming a phalanx. A military formation perfected by the army of ancient Greece, the phalanx is credited as the cornerstone of European military development. Time & Life Pictures/Getty Images

phalanx. Fully developed by the ancient Greeks, it survived in modified form into the gunpowder era and is viewed today as the beginning of European military development.

The ancient Sumerian army fielded a standard six-man-deep phalanx; the first line went into battle carrying large, rectangular shields, and the troops bore heavy pikes and battle axes. During the 7th century BCE the Greek city-states adopted a phalanx eight men deep. The Greek hoplite, the heavy-armed infantryman who manned the phalanx, was equipped with a round shield, a heavy corselet of leather and metal, greaves (shin armour), a 2.5-metre (8-foot) pike for thrusting, and a 60-cm (2-foot) double-edged sword. Since the phalanx held in solid ranks and was divided only into the centre and wings, there was generally little need for an officer corps; the whole line advanced in step to the sound of the flute. Such a formation encouraged cohesion among advancing troops and presented a frightening spectacle to the enemy, but it was difficult to maneuver and, if penetrated by enemy formations, became little more than a mob.

The basic Greek formation was made more flexible by Philip II of Macedon and his son, Alexander III the Great. Alexander's core unit in the phalanx was the syntagma, normally 16 men deep. Each soldier was armed with the sarissa, a 4- to 6-metre (13- to 21-foot) spear. In battle formation, the first five ranks held their spears horizontally in front of the advancing phalanx, each file being practically on the heels of the men in front. The remaining 11 ranks presumably held their spears vertically or rested them on the shoulders of those in front. On both sides of the syntagma, lending mobility as well as protection, was the light infantry, a disciplined force of archers, slingers, and javelin men. Protecting the flanks and poised to charge the enemy's weak points was heavy cavalry, armed with sword and javelin. Squadrons of light horse were used for scouting and skirmishing.

From the founding of their city-state until the close of the 2nd century BCE, the Romans found the Greek-style phalanx suitable for fighting in the plains of Latium. The basic weapon for this formation was a thrusting spear called the *hasta*; from this the heavy infantry derived its name, *hastati*. However, as the Roman Republic expanded, the phalanx formation was found to be too unwieldy for fragmented fighting in the hills and valleys of central Italy. Accordingly, the Romans evolved a new tactical system based on small and supple infantry units called maniples. Each maniple numbered 120 men in 12 files and 10 ranks. Maniples drew up for battle in three lines, each line made up of 10 maniples and the whole arranged in a checkerboard pattern. Separating each unit was an interval equivalent to a maniple's front of 18 metres (60 feet), so that the maniples of the first line could fall back in defense into the intervals of the second line. Conversely, the second line could merge with the first to form a solid front 10 ranks deep and 360 metres (1,200 feet) wide. In the third line, 10 maniples of light infantry were supplemented by smaller units of reserves. The three lines were 75 metres (250 feet) apart, and from front to rear one maniple of each line formed a cohort of 420 men; this was the Roman equivalent of a battalion. Ten cohorts made up the heavy-infantry strength of a legion, which was the largest permanent organization in the armies of ancient Rome. Twenty cohorts were usually combined with a small cavalry force and other supporting units into a little self-supporting army of about 10,000 men.

Two infantry weapons gave the legion its famous flexibility and force: the *pilum,* a 2-metre (7-foot) javelin used for both throwing and thrusting, and the *gladius,* a 50-cm (20-inch) cut-and-thrust sword with a broad, heavy blade. For protection, each legionary had a metal helmet, cuirass, and convex shield. In battle, the first line of maniples attacked on the double, hurling javelins and then diving in with swords before the enemy had time to recover. Then came the maniples of the second line, and only a resolute foe could rally from the two successive shocks.

As Roman armies of the late Republic and Empire became larger and more professional, the cohort, with an average field strength of 360 men, replaced the maniple as the chief tactical unit within legions. In the military operations of Lucius Cornelius Sulla and Julius Caesar, a legion was composed of 10 cohorts, with four cohorts in the first line and three each in the second and third lines.

The 3,600 heavy infantry were supported by enough cavalry and light infantry to bring the legion's strength up to 6,000 men. Seven legions in three lines, comprising about 25,000 heavy infantry, occupied a mile and a half of front.

As Rome evolved from a conquering to a defending power, the cohort was increased to a field strength of 500–600 men. These still depended on the shock tactics of *pilum* and *gladius,* but the 5,000–6,000 heavy infantry in a legion were now combined with an equal number of supporting cavalry troops and light infantry made up of archers, slingers, and javelin men. In order to deal with mounted barbarian raiders, the proportion of cavalry rose from one-seventh to one-fourth. By the 4th century CE, with the empire defending its many fortified border outposts, as many as 10 catapults and 60 ballistae were assigned to each legion.

MILITARY TECHNOLOGY OF THE PERIOD

Perhaps the strongest underlying technological feature of the earliest periods of military history was the heavy reliance on human muscle, which retained a tactical primacy that contrasted starkly with medieval times, when the application of horse power became a prime ingredient of victory. Heavy infantry remained the dominant European military institution until it was overthrown in the 4th century CE by a system of war in which shock cavalry played the central role.

There were two major, if partial, exceptions to this prevailing feature: the success of horse archers in the great Eurasian Steppe during late classical times and the decisive use in the 4th century BCE of shock cavalry by the armies of Philip II of Macedon and his son Alexander the Great. However, the defeat of Roman legions by Parthian horse archers at Carrhae in western Mesopotamia in 53 BCE marked merely a shifting of boundaries between ecospheres on topographical grounds rather than any fundamental change within the core of the European ecosphere itself. Also, the shock cavalry of Philip and Alexander was an exception so rare as to prove the rule; moreover, their decisiveness was made possible by the power of the Macedonian infantry phalanx.

Classical technologists never developed an efficient means of applying animal traction to haulage on land, no doubt because agricultural resources in even the most advanced areas were incapable of supporting meaningful numbers of horses powerful enough to make the effort worthwhile. Carts were heavy and easily broken, and the throat-and-girth harness for horses, mules, and donkeys put pressure on the animals' windpipes and neck veins, severely restricting the amount they could pull. The yoke-and-pole harness for oxen was relatively efficient and oxen could pull heavy loads, but they were extremely slow. A human porter, on the other hand, was just as efficient as a pack horse in weight carried per unit of food consumed. The best recipe for mobility, therefore, was to restrict pack animals to the minimum needed for carrying bulky items such as essential rations, tents, and firewood, to use carts only for items such as siege engines that could be carried in no other way, and to require soldiers to carry all their personal equipment and some of their food.

On the other hand, mastery of wood and bronze for military purposes reached a level during this period that was seldom, if ever, attained afterward. Surviving patterns for the Roman military boot, the caliga, suggest equally high standards of craftsmanship in leatherworking, and the standards of carpentry displayed on classical ships were almost impossibly high when measured against those of later eras.

DEFENSIVE WEAPONRY

The design and production of individual defensive equipment was restricted by the shape of the human form that it had to protect; at the same time, it placed heavy demands on the smith's skills. The large areas to be protected, restrictions on the weight that a combatant could carry, the difficulty of forging metal into the complex contours required, and cost all conspired to force constant change.

The technology of defensive weapons was rarely static. Evidence exists of an ancient contest between offensive and defensive weaponry, with defensive weaponry at first leading the way. By 3000

BCE Mesopotamian smiths had learned to craft helmets of copper-and-arsenic bronze, which, no doubt worn with a well-padded leather lining, largely neutralized the offensive advantages of the mace. By 2500 BCE the Sumerians were making helmets of bronze, along with bronze spearheads and ax blades. The weapon smiths' initial response to the helmet was to augment the crushing power of the mace by casting the head in an ellipsoidal form that concentrated more force at the point of impact. Then, as technical competence increased, the ellipsoidal head became a cutting edge, and by this process the mace evolved into the ax. The contest between mace and helmet initiated a contest between offensive and defensive technology that continued throughout history.

HELMETS

The helmet, though arguably the earliest focus of the armourer's craft, was one of the most demanding challenges. Forging an integral, one-piece dome of metal capable of covering the entire head was extremely difficult. The Corinthian Greek helmet, a deep, bowl-shaped helmet of carefully graduated thickness forged from a single piece of bronze, probably represented the functional as well as aesthetic apex of the bronze worker's art. Many classical Greek helmets of bronze were joined by a seam down the crown.

Iron helmets followed the evolution of iron mail, itself a sophisticated and relatively late development. The legionnaire

A Corinthian bronze helmet, believed to date back to at least the 1st century BCE. DEA/A. De Gregorio/De Agostini Picture Library/Getty Images

of the early Roman Republic wore a helmet of bronze, while his successor in the Empire of the 1st century CE wore one of iron.

SHIELDS

Shields were used for hunting long before they were used for warfare, partly for defense and partly for concealment in stalking game; it is likely that the military shield evolved from that of the hunter and herdsman. The size and composition of shields varied greatly, depending on the tactical demands of the user. In general, the more effective the protection afforded by body armour, the smaller the shield. Similarly, the longer the reach of the soldier's weapon, the smaller his shield.

The Greek hoplite, a heavy infantryman who fought in closely packed formation, acquired his name from the *hoplon*, a convex, circular shield, approximately 90 cm (3 feet) in diameter, made of composite wood and bronze. It was carried on the left arm by means of a bronze strap that passed across the forearm and a rope looped around the inner rim with sufficient slack to be gripped in the fist. In the 4th century BCE the soldier of the Roman Republic, who fought primarily with the spear, carried an oval shield, while the later imperial legionnaire, who closed in with a short sword, protected himself with the *scutum*, a large cylindrical shield of leather-clad wood that covered most of his body.

BODY ARMOUR

Padded garments, and perhaps armour of hardened leather, preceded edged metal weapons. It was then a logical, if expensive, step to cast or forge small metal plates and sew them onto a protective garment. These provided real protection against arrow, spear, or mace, and the small scales, perforated for attachment, were a far less demanding technical challenge than even the simplest helmet. Armour of overlapping scales of bronze, laced together or sewn onto a backing of padded fabric,

is well represented in pictorial evidence and burial items from Mesopotamia, Palestine, and Egypt from about 1500 BCE, though its use was probably restricted to a small elite.

Bronze

By classical times, breastplates of bronze, at first beaten and then cast to the warrior's individual shape, were commonplace among heavy infantry and elite cavalry. Greaves, defenses for the lower leg, closely followed the breastplate. At first these were forged of bronze plates; some classical Greek examples were cast to such fine tolerances that they sprang open and could be snapped onto the calf. Defenses for more remote portions of the body, such as vambraces for the forearm and defenses for the ankle resembling spats, were included in Greek temple dedications, but they were probably not common in field service.

Bronze was the most common metal for body defenses well into the Iron Age, a consequence of the fact that it could be worked in large pieces without extended hand forging and careful tempering, while iron had to be forged from relatively small billets.

Mail

The first practical body armour of iron was mail, which made its appearance in Hellenistic times but became common only during the Roman Imperial period. (Bronze mail was impractical because

TYPES OF ARMOUR

Types of armour generally fall into one of three main categories: (1) armour made of leather, fabric, or mixed layers of both, sometimes reinforced by quilting or felt, (2) mail, made of interwoven rings of iron or steel, and (3) rigid armour made of metal, horn, wood, plastic, or some other similar tough and resistant material. The third category includes the plate armour that protected the knights of Europe in the Middle Ages. This armour was composed of large steel or iron plates that were linked by loosely closed rivets and by internal leathers to allow the wearer maximum freedom of movement.

Presumably, the use of armour extends back beyond historical records, when primitive warriors protected themselves with leather hides and helmets. In the 11th century BCE, Chinese warriors wore armour made of five to seven layers of rhinoceros skin, and ox hides were similarly used by the Mongols in the 13th century CE. Fabric armour too has a long history, with thick, multilayered linen cuirasses (armour covering the body from neck to waist) worn by the Greek heavy infantry of the 5th century BCE and quilted linen coats worn in northern India until the 19th century.

of the insufficient strength of the alloy.) Mail, or chain mail, was made of small rings of iron, typically of one-half-inch diameter or less, linked into a protective fabric. The rings were fastened together in patterns of varying complexity depending on the degree of protection desired; in general, smaller, lighter rings fastened in dense, overlapping patterns meant lighter, better protection. The fabrication of mail was extremely labour-intensive. The earliest mail was made of handforged links, each individual link riveted together. Later, armourers used punches of hardened iron to cut rings from sheets. This reduced the labour involved and, hence, the cost.

The earliest evidence of mail is depicted on Greek sculpture and friezes dating from the 3rd century BCE, though this kind of protection might be considerably older (there was some evidence that it might be of Celtic origin). Little else is known about the use of mail by the Greeks, but the Roman legionnaire was equipped with a *lorica hamata*, a mail shirt, from a very early date. Mail was extremely flexible and provided good protection against cutting and piercing weapons. Its main disadvantage was its weight, which tended to hang from the shoulders and waist. In addition, strips of mail tended to curl at the edges; the Romans solved this problem by lacing mail shoulder defenses to leather plates. In the 1st century CE the legionnaire's mail shirt gave way to a segmented iron torso defense, the *lorica segmentata*.

Plate-Iron Armour

While some early forged bronze armour was technically plate, the introduction of the *lorica segmentata* heralded the production of practical plate armour on a large scale. In general, the term *plate* would imply a uniform thickness of metal, and only iron could provide reasonably effective protection with uniform thickness without excessive weight.

While the Republican legionnaire's *lorica hamata* hung to the midthigh, his imperial successor's *lorica segmentata* covered only the shoulders and torso. On the whole, classical plate armour probably provided better protection against smashing and heavy piercing blows, while a shirt of well-made mail covered more of the body and, hence, afforded better protection against slashing blows and missiles.

OFFENSIVE WEAPONRY

Development of the offensive technology of war was not as constrained by technological and economic limitations as was defensive weaponry. Every significant offensive weapon was widely available, while defensive equipment of high quality was almost always confined to the elite. Perhaps as a consequence, a wide variety of individual offensive weapons appeared in antiquity. One of the most striking facets of ancient military technology is the early date by which individual weapons attained their form and the longevity of early offensive weapons concepts. Some of the weapons of antiquity disappeared as practical military implements in classical and medieval times, and all underwent modification, but, with the exception of the halberd and crossbow, virtually every significant pre-gunpowder weapon was known in antiquity.

THE AX

Limitations on the strength of bronze and difficulties in casting and hafting restricted the ax at first to a relatively broad blade mortised into a handle at three points and secured with bindings or rivets. The hafting problem became acute as improvements in armour dictated longer, narrower blades designed primarily for piercing rather than cutting. This led to the development of socketed axes, in which the handle passed through a tubular hole cast in the ax head; both hole and head were tapered from front to rear to prevent the head from flying off. This far stronger hafting technique must have been accompanied by a significant improvement in the quality of the metal itself. The pace and timing of these developments varied enormously from place to place, depending on the local level of technology. Sumerian smiths were casting socketed ax heads with narrow piercing blades by 2500 BCE, while simple mortise-and-tenon hafting was still being used in Egypt 1,000 years later.

THE SPEAR

Though early man probably employed spears of fire-hardened wood, spearheads of knapped stone were used long before the emergence of any distinction between hunting and military weapons. Bronze spearheads closely followed the development of alloys hard enough to keep a cutting edge and represented, with the piercing ax, the earliest significant military application of bronze. Spearheads were also among the earliest militarily significant applications of iron, no doubt because existing patterns could be directly extrapolated from bronze to iron. Though the hafting is quite different, bronze Sumerian spearheads of the 3rd millennium BCE differ only marginally in shape from the leaf-shaped spearheads of classical Greece.

The spears of antiquity were relatively short, commonly less than the height of the warrior, and typically were wielded with one hand. As defensive armour and other weapons of shock combat (notably the sword) improved, spear shafts were made longer and the use of the spear became more specialized. The Greek hoplite's spear was a little less than 3 metres (about 9 feet) long. The Macedonian *sarissa* was twice that length in the period of Alexander's conquests and it grew to some 6 metres (21 feet) in Hellenistic times.

THE JAVELIN

Javelins, or throwing spears, were shorter and lighter than spears designed for shock combat and had smaller heads. The distinction between javelin and spear was slow to develop, but by classical times the heavy spear was clearly distinguished from the javelin, and specialized javelin troops were commonly used for skirmishing. A throwing string was sometimes looped around the shaft and tied to the thrower's finger to impart spin to the javelin on release. This improved the weapon's accuracy and probably increased the range and penetrating power by permitting a harder cast.

A significant refinement of the javelin was the Roman pilum. The pilum was relatively short, about 1.5 metres (5 feet) long, and had a heavy head of soft iron that made up nearly one-third of the weapon's total length. The weight of this weapon restricted its range but gave it greater impact. Its head of soft iron was intended to bend on impact, preventing an enemy from throwing it back.

Like the spear, the javelin was relatively unaffected by the appearance of iron and retained its characteristic form until it was finally abandoned as a serious weapon in the 16th century.

THE SLING

The sling was the simplest of the missile weapons of antiquity in principle and the most difficult in practice. It consisted of two cords or thongs fastened to a pouch. A small stone was placed in the pouch, and the slinger whirled the whole affair around to build up velocity before letting go of one of the cord ends to release the projectile. While considerable velocity could be imparted to a projectile in this way, the geometry of the scheme dictated that the release be timed with uncanny precision to achieve even rudimentary accuracy. Almost always wielded by tribal or regionally recruited specialists who acquired their skills in youth, the sling featured prominently in warfare in antiquity and classical times. It outranged the javelin and even—at least at some times and places—the bow (a point confirmed in the 4th century BCE by the Greek historian Xenophon). By classical times, lead bullets, often with slogans or epigrams cast into them—"A nasty present!"—were used as projectiles.

The sling vanished as a weapon of war in the Old World by the end of the classical period, owing mainly to the disappearance of the tribal cultures in which it originated. (In the New World, on the other hand, both the Aztecs and Incas used the sling with great effect against Spanish conquistadores in the 16th century.)

THE SWORD

The advantages of a long, sharp blade had to await advanced smelting and

Rudimentary slings such as this, used to turn stones into deadly projectiles, were common weapons wielded in battle during antiquity and classical times. © James Steidl/SuperFusion/SuperStock

casting technology before they could be realized. By about 1500 BCE the cutting ax had evolved into the sickle sword, a bronze sword with a curved, concave blade and a straight, thickened handle. Bronze swords with straight blades more than .91 metre (3 feet) long have been found in Greek grave sites; however, because this length exceeded the structural capabilities of bronze, these swords were not practical weapons. As a serious military implement, the sword had to await the development of iron forging, and the first true swords date from about 1200 BCE.

Swords in antiquity and classical times tended to be relatively short, at first because they were made of bronze and later because they were rarely called upon to penetrate iron armour. The blade of the classic Roman stabbing sword, the *gladius*, was only .60 metre (2 feet) long, though in the twilight years of the empire the *gladius* gave way to the spatha, the long slashing sword of the barbarians.

THE BOW

The bow was simple in concept, yet it represented an extremely sophisticated technology. In its most basic form, the bow consisted of a stave of wood slightly bent by the tension of a bowstring connecting its two ends. The bow stored the force of the archer's draw as potential energy, then transferred it to the bowstring as kinetic energy, imparting velocity and killing power to the arrow. The bow could store no more energy than the archer was capable of producing in a single movement of the muscles of his back and arms, but it released the stored energy at a higher velocity, thus overcoming the arm's inherent limitations.

Though not as evident, the sophistication of arrow technology matched that of the bow. The effectiveness of the bow depended on the arrow's efficiency in retaining kinetic energy throughout its trajectory and then transforming it into killing power on impact. This was not a simple problem, as it depended on the mass, aerodynamic drag, and stability of the arrow and on the hardness and shape of the head. These factors were related to one another and to the characteristics of the bow in a complex calculus. The most important variables in this calculus were arrow weight and the length and stiffness of the bow.

Assuming the same length of draw and available force, the total amount of potential energy that an archer could store in a bow was a function of the bow's length; that is, the longer the arms of the bow, the more energy stored per unit of work expended in the draw and, therefore, the more kinetic energy imparted to the string and arrow. The disadvantage of a long bow was that the stored energy had to serve not only to drive the string and arrow but also to accelerate the mass of the bow itself. Because the longer bow's more massive arms accelerated more slowly, a longer bow imparted kinetic energy to the string and arrow at a lower velocity. A shorter bow, on the

ARROWS

Arrow design was probably the first area of military technology in which production consid-erations assumed overriding importance. As a semi-expendable munition that was used in quantity, arrows could not be evaluated solely by their technological effectiveness; production costs had to be considered as well. As a consequence, the materials used for arrowheads tended to be a step behind those used for other offensive technologies. Arrowheads of flint and obsid-ian, knapped to remarkably uniform standards, survived well into the Bronze Age, and bronze arrowheads were used long after the adoption of iron for virtually every other military cutting or piercing implement.

Arrow shafts were made of relatively inexpensive wood and reed throughout history, though considerable labour was involved in shaping them. Remarkably refined techniques for fastening arrowheads of flint and obsidian to shafts were well in hand long before recorded history. The importance of arrow manufacturing techniques is reflected in the survival in modern English of the given name Fletcher, the title of a specialist in attaching feathers to the arrow shaft.

other hand, stored less energy for the same amount of work expended in the draw, but it compensated for this through its ability to transmit the energy to the arrow at a higher velocity. In sum, the shorter bow imparted less total energy to the arrow, but it did so at a higher velocity. Therefore, in practice maximum range was attained by a short, stiff bow shooting a very light arrow, and maxi-mum killing power at medium ranges was attained by a long bow driving a rela-tively heavy arrow.

The Early Bow

The simple bow, made from a single piece of wood, was known to Neolithic hunters; it is clearly depicted in cave paintings of 30,000 BCE and earlier. The first improve-ment was the reflex bow, a bow that was curved forward, or reflexively, near its centre so that the string lay close against the grip before the bow was drawn. This increased the effective length of the draw since it began farther forward, close to the archer's left hand.

The Composite Recurved Bow

The next major improvement, one that was to remain preeminent among missile weapons until well into the modern era, was the composite recurved bow. This development overcame the inherent limi-tations of wood in stiffness and tensile strength. The composite bow's resistance to bending was increased by reinforcing the rear, or belly, of the bow with horn; its speed and power in recoil were increased by overlaying the front of the bow with sinew, usually applied under tension. The wooden structure of this composite thus consisted of little more than thin wooden strips supporting the horn and sinew. The more powerful composite bows, being very highly stressed, reversed their curvature when unstrung. They acquired the name recurved since the outer arms of the bow curved away from the archer when the bow was strung, which imparted a mechanical advantage at the end of the draw. Monumental and artistic evidence suggest that the principle of the composite recurved bow was known as early as 3000 BCE.

A prime advantage of the composite bow was that it could be engineered to essentially any desired strength. By following the elaborate but empirically understood trade-off between length and stiffness referred to above, the bowyer could produce a short bow capable of propelling light arrows to long ranges, a long, heavy bow designed to maximize penetrative power at relatively short ranges, or any desired compromise between.

MECHANICAL ARTILLERY

In contrast to individual weaponry, there was little continuity from classical to medieval times in mechanical artillery. The only exception—and it may have been a case of independent reinvention—was the similarity of the Roman onager to the medieval catapult.

Mechanical artillery of classical times was of two types: tension and torsion. In the first, energy to drive the projectile was provided by the tension of a drawn bow. In the other, it was provided by torsional energy stored in bundles of twisted fibres.

The invention of mechanical artillery was ascribed traditionally to the initiative of Dionysius I, tyrant of Syracuse, in Sicily, who in 399 BCE directed his engineers to construct military engines in preparation for war with Carthage. Dionysius' engineers surely drew on existing practice. The earliest of the Greek engines was the gastrophetes, or "belly shooter." In effect a large crossbow, it received its name because the user braced the stock against his belly to draw the weapon. Though Greek texts did not go into detail on construction of the bow, it was based on a composite bow of wood, horn, and sinew.

The potential of such engines was apparent, and the demand for greater power and range quickly exceeded the capabilities of tension. By the middle of the 3rd century BCE, the bow had been replaced by rigid wooden arms constrained in a wooden box and drawn against the force of tightly twisted bundles of hair or sinew. The overall concept was similar to the gastrophetes, but the substitution of torsion for tension permitted larger and more powerful engines to be made. Such catapults (from Greek kata, "to pierce," and pelte, "shield"; a "shield piercer") could throw a javelin as far as 700 metres (800 yards). The same basic principle was applied to large stone-throwing engines. The Jewish historian Josephus referred to Roman catapults used in the siege of Jerusalem in

70 CE that could throw a one-talent stone (about 25 kg, or 55 pounds) two *stades* (360 metres, or 400 yards) or more.

The terminology of mechanical artillery is confusing. *Catapult* is the general term for mechanical artillery. However, the term also narrowly applies to a particular type of torsion engine with a single arm rotating in a vertical plane. Torsion engines with two horizontally opposed arms rotating in the horizontal plane, such as that described above, are called ballistae. There is no evidence that catapults in the narrow sense were used by the Greeks. The Romans called their catapults onagers, or wild asses, for the way in which their rears kicked upward under the recoil force. The Romans used large ballistae and onagers effectively in siege operations, and a complement of *carroballistae*, small, wheel-mounted torsion engines, was a regular part of the legion. The onager and the medieval catapult were identical in concept, but ballistae were not used after the classical era.

FORTIFICATION

Fortifications in antiquity were designed primarily to defeat attempts at escalade (scale), though cover was provided for archers and javelin throwers along the ramparts and for enfilade fire from flanking towers. By classical Greek times, fortress architecture had attained a high level of sophistication; both the profile and trace (that is, the height above ground level and the outline of the walls) of fortifications were designed to achieve overlapping fields of fire from ballistae mounted along the ramparts and in supporting towers. Roman fortresses of the 2nd century CE, largely designed for logistic and administrative convenience, tended to have square or rectangular outlines, and were situated along major communication routes. By the late 3rd century, their walls had become thicker and had flanking towers strengthened to support mechanical artillery. The number of gates was reduced, and the ditches were dug wider. By the late 4th and 5th centuries, Roman fortresses were being built on easily defensible ground with irregular outlines that conformed to the topography; clearly, passive defense had become the dominant design consideration.

In general, the quality of masonry that went into permanent defensive works of the classical period was very high by later standards. Fortifications were almost exclusively of dressed stone, though by Roman times concrete mortar was used on occasion.

The main purpose of early field fortification, particularly among the Greeks, was to secure an advantage by standing on higher ground so that the enemy was forced to attack uphill. The Romans were especially adept at field fortifications, preparing fortified camps at the close of each day's march. The troops usually required three to four hours to dig a ditch around the periphery, erect a rampart or palisade from timbers carried by each man, lay out streets, and pitch tents. During extended campaigns the Romans strengthened the camps with towers and outlying redoubts, or small forts, and used the camps as bases for offensive forays into the surrounding territory.

For breaching fortified positions, military engineers of the classical age designed assault towers that remain a wonder to modern engineers. So large was one siege tower used by Macedonians in an attack on Rhodes that 3,400 men were required to move it up to the city walls. Another 1,000 men were needed to wield a battering ram 55 metres (180 feet) long. The Romans constructed huge siege towers, one of which Caesar mentions as being 45 metres (150 feet) high. The lower stories housed the battering ram, which had either a pointed head for breaching or a ramlike head for battering. Archers in the upper stories shot arrows to drive the defenders from their ramparts. From the top of the tower, a hinged bridge might be lowered to serve a storming party. To guard the attackers against enemy missiles, the Romans used great wicker or wooden shields, called mantelets, which were sometimes mounted on wheels. In some cases the attackers might approach the fortress under the protection of wooden galleries.

LAND TRANSPORTATION

In antiquity and classical times the transportation technology of land warfare largely amounted to man's own powers of locomotion. This was due in part to limitations in the size, strength, and stamina of horses and in part to deficiencies in

Warriors utilizing a siege tower in their attack on an English castle. The illustration is taken from a book on British history by William Aubrey, published in the late 1800s. Universal Images Group/ Hulton Archive/Getty Images

crucial supporting technologies, notably the inefficiency of harnesses for horses and nonpivoting front axles for wagons. A more basic underlying factor was the generally low level of economic development. The horse was an economically inefficient animal, consuming large quantities of food. Of more importance, keeping horses—let alone selectively breeding them for size, strength, and power—was a highly labour-intensive and capital-intensive enterprise for which the classical world was not organized. An efficient pulling harness for horses was unknown, and mules and donkeys fitted with carrying baskets, or panniers, balanced in pairs across the back, were the most common pack or dray animals. The ox, the heavy-duty dray animal of the Mediterranean world, was used for military purposes when heavy loads were involved and speed was not critical.

THE HORSE

Because it was not possible to maintain a breed of war-horses sufficiently powerful to sustain mounted shock action, the horse was restricted to a subsidiary role in warfare from the eclipse of the chariot in the middle of the 2nd millennium BCE until the rise of the horse archer in the 4th century CE. Evidence as to the size of horses in classical times is equivocal. Greek vase paintings from the 7th century BCE depict Scythians riding tall, apparently powerful horses with long, slender legs, implying speed; however, this breed evidently collapsed and disappeared. Later Mongolian steppe ponies, though tough and tractable, were probably considerably smaller.

Horses were rarely if ever used for drayage. This was partly because their rarity and expense restricted them to combat roles, and partly because of the lack of a suitable harness. The prevalent harness consisted of a pole-and-yoke assembly, attached to the animal by neck and chest harness. This was developed for use with oxen, where the primary load was absorbed by the thrust of the animal's hump against

the yoke. With a horse, most of the pulling load was borne by the neck strap, which tended to strangle the horse and constrict blood flow.

THE ELEPHANT

The war elephant was first used in India and was known to the Persians by the 4th century BCE. Though they accomplished little subsequently, their presence in Hannibal's army during its transit of the Alps into Italy in 218 BCE underscored their perceived utility. The elephant's tactical importance apparently stemmed in large part from its willingness to charge both men and horses and from the panic that it inspired in horses.

THE CHARIOT

The chariot was the earliest means of transportation in combat other than man's own powers of locomotion. The earliest known chariots, shown in Sumerian depictions from about 2500 BCE, were not true chariots but four-wheeled carts with solid wooden wheels drawn by a team of four donkeys or wild asses. They were no doubt heavy and cumbersome; lacking a pivoting front axle, they would have skidded through turns.

Around 1600 BCE Iranian tribes introduced the war-horse into Mesopotamia from the north, along with the light two-wheeled chariot. The Hyksos apparently introduced the chariot into Egypt shortly thereafter, by which time it was a mature technology. By the middle of the 2nd millennium BCE, Egyptian, Hittite, and Palestinian chariots were extraordinarily light and flexible vehicles, the wheels and tires in particular exhibiting great sophistication in design and fabrication. Light war chariots were drawn by either two or three horses, which were harnessed by means of chest girths secured by one or two poles and a yoke.

That horses were long used for pulling chariots rather than for riding is probably attributable to the horse's inadequate strength and incomplete domestication. The chariot was subject to mechanical failure and, more important, was immobilized when any one of its horses was incapacitated. Moreover, the art of riding astride in cavalry fashion had been mastered long before the chariot's eclipse as a tactically dominant weapon. The decline of the chariot by the end of the 2nd millennium BCE was probably related to the spread of iron weaponry, but it was surely related also to the breeding of horses with sufficient strength and stamina to carry an armed man. Chariots lingered in areas of slower technological advance, but in the classical world they were retained mainly for ceremonial functions.

CHAPTER 2

WAR IN THE MIDDLE AGES

The period of European history extending from about 500 to 1400–1500 CE is traditionally known as the Middle Ages. Although once regarded as a time of uninterrupted ignorance, superstition, and social oppression, the Middle Ages are now understood as a dynamic period during which political, social, economic, and cultural structures were profoundly reorganized. This was as true in warfare as it was in society. Beginning with the unchallenged superiority of the noble cavalryman, the Middle Ages ended with the rise of the burgher and yeoman fighting on foot with pike, halberd, and crossbow.

THE AGE OF CAVALRY

The beginning of the age of cavalry in Europe is traditionally dated to the destruction of the legions of the Roman emperor Valens by Gothic horsemen at the Battle of Adrianople in 378 CE. The period that followed, characterized by the network of political and economic relationships called feudalism, was an age during which the mounted arm assumed an ascendancy that it began to relinquish only in the 14th century, with the appearance of infantry capable of taking the open field unsupported against mounted chivalry.

Cavalry, however, was only part of the story of this era. However impressive the mounted knight may have been in battle, he required a secure place of replenishment and refuge. This was provided by the seigneurial fortress, or castle. In a military sense, European feudalism rested on a symbiotic relationship between armoured man-at-arms, war-horse, and castle.

THE MEDIEVAL KNIGHT

In the modern era the English word *knight* (in French, *chevalier*, and in German, *Ritter*) is a title of honour bestowed on a person for a variety of services, but originally in the Middle Ages it was reserved for a formally professed cavalryman. Some knights were vassals holding lands as fiefs from the lords in whose armies they served, while others were not enfeoffed with land. The process of entering knighthood often became formalized. A youth destined for the profession of arms might from the age of 7 or so serve his father as a page before joining the household of his father's suzerain, perhaps at the age of 12, for more advanced instruction not only in military subjects but also in the ways of the world. During this period of his apprenticeship he would be known as a damoiseau (literally "lordling"), or varlet, or *valet* (German: *Knappe*), until he followed his patron on a campaign as his shieldbearer, *écuyer,* or esquire, or as the bearer of his weapons (armiger). When he was adjudged proficient and the money was forthcoming for the purchase of his knightly equipment, he would be dubbed knight.

The ceremonial of dubbing varied considerably. It might be highly elaborate on a great feast day or on a royal occasion, or it could be simply performed on the battlefield; the dubbing knight might use any appropriate formula that he liked. A common element, however, was the use of the flat of a swordblade for a touch on the shoulder—i.e., the accolade of knighthood as it survives in modern times.

As knighthood evolved, a Christian ideal of knightly behaviour came to be accepted, involving respect for the church, protection of the poor and the weak, loyalty to one's feudal or military superiors, and preservation of personal honour. The nearest that the ideal ever came to realization, however, was in the Crusades, which, from the end of the 11th century, brought the knights of Christian Europe together in a common enterprise under the auspices of the church. Knights dubbed at Christ's tomb were known as knights of the Holy Sepulchre. During the Crusades the first orders of knights came into being: the Hospitallers of St. John of Jerusalem (later the Knights of Malta); the Order of the Temple of Solomon (Templars); and, rather later, the Order of St. Lazarus, which had a special duty of protecting leper hospitals. These orders were truly international and of an expressly religious nature both in their purpose and in their form, with celibacy for their members and a hierarchical structure (grand master; "pillars" of lands, or provincial masters; grand priors; commanders; knights) resembling that of the church itself. But it was not long before their religious aim gave place to political activity as the orders grew in numbers and in wealth.

At the same time, crusading orders with a rather more national bias came into being. In Spain, for the struggle against the Muslims there or for the protection of pilgrims, the Orders of Calatrava and

Knight in Gothic armour, 15th-century woodcut. Rosenwald Collection—Rare Book/Special Collections Reading Room/Library of Congress, Washington D.C. (LC Control No.: 48042317)

of Alcántara and Santiago (St. James) were founded in Castile between 1156 and 1171. Portugal had the Order of Avís, founded about the same time, but Aragon's Order of Montesa (1317) and Portugal's Order of Christ were not founded until after the dissolution of the Templars. The greatest order of German knights was the Teutonic Order. These "national" crusading orders followed a course of worldly aggrandizement like that of the international orders, but the crusades in Europe that they undertook, no less than the international enterprises in Palestine, would long attract individual knights from abroad or from outside their ranks.

Between the end of the 11th century and the middle of the 13th, a change took place in the relationship of knighthood to feudalism. The feudal host, whose knights were enfeoffed landholders obliged to give 40 days' service per year normally, had been adequate for defense and for service within a kingdom; but it was scarcely appropriate for the now more frequent long-distance expeditions of the time, whether crusades or sustained invasions such as those launched in the Anglo-French wars. The result was twofold. On the one hand, the kings often resorted to distraint of knighthood, that is, to compelling holders of land above a certain value to come and be dubbed knights. On the other hand, the armies came to be composed more and more largely of mercenary soldiers, with the knights, who had once formed the main body of the combatants, reduced to a minority—as it were to a class of officers.

The gradual demise of the Crusades, the disastrous defeats of knightly armies by foot soldiers and bowmen, the development of artillery, the steady erosion of feudalism by the royal power in favour of centralized monarchy—all these factors spelled the disintegration of traditional knighthood in the 14th and 15th centuries. Knighthood lost its martial purpose and, by the 16th century, had been reduced to an honorific status that sovereigns could bestow as they pleased. It became a fashion of modish elegance for the sophisticated nobles of a prince's entourage.

MAIL ARMOUR

The availability of high-quality iron armour, particularly mail, to mounted warrior elites was instrumental in the fall of Rome and the establishment of European feudalism. Until the 10th century, however, there was little qualitative difference between the body armour of the western European knight and the Roman legionnaire's *lorica hamata*. Then, during the 11th century, the sleeves of the knight's mail shirt, or byrnie, became longer and closer-fitting, extending downward from the middle of the upper arm to the wrist; at the same time, the hem of the byrnie dropped from just above to just below the kneecap. Knights began wearing the gambeson, a quilted garment of leather or canvas, beneath their mail for additional protection and to cushion the shock of blows. (Ordinary soldiers often wore a gambeson as their only protection.) Use of the surcoat, a light garment worn over the knight's armour, became general during this period. Both gambeson and surcoat may have been Arab imports, adopted as a result of exposure to Muslim technology during the Crusades.

Norman men-at-arms were protected by a knee-length mail shirt called a hauberk, which was a later version of the Saxon byrnie that was split to permit the wearer to sit astride his horse. Though 11th-century men-at-arms probably did not have complete mail trousers, the hauberk apparently had inserts of cloth or leather, giving the same effect. It also included a hoodlike garment of mail worn over the head to protect the neck and throat; this had a hole for the face much like a modern ski cap. The hood was backed by padding of cloth or leather, and a pointed iron helmet with nasal (a vertical bar protecting the nose) was worn over it. The knight's defensive equipment was completed by a large, kite-shaped shield, nearly two-thirds the height of its owner. The size of this shield was testimony to the incomplete protection offered by the hauberk.

During the 12th century the open helmet with nasal evolved into the pot helm, or casque. This was an involved process, with the crown of the helmet losing its pointed shape to become flat and the nasal expanding to cover the entire face except for small vision slits and breathing holes. The late 12th-century helm was typically a barrel-shaped affair;

more sophisticated designs with hinged visors appeared as well. The helm was extremely heavy, and the entire weight was borne by the neck; for this reason it was only donned immediately before combat. Some knights preferred a mail coif, no doubt with heavy padding and perhaps an iron cap beneath. One 12th-century depiction shows an iron visor worn over a coif of mail.

By the early 13th century European amourers had learned to make mail with a sufficiently fine mesh to provide protection to the hand. At first this was in the form of mittens with a leather-lined hole in the palm through which the knight could thrust his hand when out of action; by mid-century the armourer's skill had developed to the point of making complete gloves of mail.

PLATE ARMOUR

The earliest knightly plate armour appeared shortly after 1200 in the form of thin plates worn beneath the gambeson. External plate armour began to appear around the middle of the century, at first for elbows, kneecaps, and shins. The true plate cuirass appeared about 1250, though it was at first unwieldy, covering only the front of the torso and no doubt placing considerable stress on the underlying garments to which it was attached. Perhaps in part for this reason, the breastplate was followed shortly by the backplate. From the late 13th century, plate protection spread from the knees and elbows to encompass the extremities. Square plates called ailettes, which protected the shoulder, made a brief appearance between about 1290 and 1325 before giving way to jointed plate defenses that covered the gap between breastplate and upper-arm defenses. Helmets with hinged visors appeared about 1300, and by mid-century armourers were constructing closed, visored helms that rested directly on the shoulder defenses. Plate armour, at first worn above mail as reinforcement, began to replace it entirely except in areas such as the crotch, the armpits, and the back of the knees, where the armourer's skill could not devise a sufficiently flexible joint. In response to this enhanced coverage, the knight's large, kite-shaped shield evolved into a much smaller implement.

The first suits of full plate armour date from the first decades of the 15th century. By 1440 the Gothic style of plate armour was well developed, representing the ultimate development of personal armour protection. Armourers were making gloves with individually jointed fingers, and shoulder defenses had become particularly sophisticated, permitting the man-at-arms full freedom to wield sword, lance, or mace with a minimum of exposure. Also during the 15th century the weight of personal armour increased, partly because of the importance of shock tactics in European warfare and partly because of the demands of jousting, a form of mock combat in which two armoured knights, separated by a low fence or barrier, rode at each other head-on and attempted to unseat each other with blunted lances. As armour

protection became more complete and heavier, larger breeds of horses appeared. Mail protection for horses became common in the 13th century; by the 15th, plate horse armour was used extensively.

The unprecedented protection that plate armour gave the man-at-arms did not come without tactical, as well as economic, cost. A closed helm seriously interfered with vision and made voice communication in battle impossible. No doubt in response to this, heraldry emerged during this period and the armorial surcoat became a standard item of knightly dress. Ultimately, the thickness of iron needed to stop missiles—at first arrows and crossbow bolts, then harquebus and musket balls—made armour so heavy as to be impractical for active service. By the 16th century, armour was largely ceremonial and decorative, with increasingly elaborate ornamentation.

THE WAR-HORSE

The destrier, or medieval war-horse, was central to the tactical viability of European feudalism. This animal was a product of two great migrations of horses originating in Central Asia. One, moving westward, crossed into Europe and there originated the vast herds of primeval animals that eventually roamed almost the entire continent. The second flowed to the southwest and found its way into Asia Minor and the neighbouring lands of Persia, India, and Arabia. Ultimately it crossed into Egypt, then spread from that country along all of North Africa. At the same time it crossed from Asia Minor into Greece and spread along the northern shores of the Mediterranean.

There were two channels through which the horses of Arabia and North Africa were distributed into northern Europe. One was through the conquest of the Romans across the Alps into France and the Low Countries, where, previously, descendants of the horses of Central Asia had constituted the equine population. The other channel led northward through Greece, Macedonia, and the Gothic countries into the land of the Vandals. When these barbarian peoples invaded the empire, the vast number of horses that they possessed helped them to overthrow the Romans. The era that followed witnessed the collapse of the Roman breeds and the gradual development—especially during the era of Charlemagne in the late 8th and early 9th centuries—of improved types, owing largely to the importation of Arabian stock. The most important of these was the "great horse," which originated in the Low Countries; its size and strength were required to carry the heavy load of the armoured knight. These horses, the ancestors of modern draft breeds, were bred from the largest and most powerful of the northern European horses, but there was apparently an admixture of Arabian breeds as well.

The Crusades of the 12th and 13th centuries took the nobility of Europe into the native land of the Arabian horse. The speed and agility of these light horses so impressed them that large numbers were imported into England and France. Over a long period of time the Moors took Arabian and North African horses into Spain, where they were crossed with the native stock and produced the superior breeds that were sought after by other nations. (Spanish horses were also taken to the New World, where they became the principal ancestors of the equine population of North and South America.)

The breeding, care, and maintenance of medieval war-horses, and the mastering of the skills of mounted combat, required immense amounts of time, skill, and resources. Horses strong enough to be ridden did not exist everywhere, and European horses in particular tended to revert in a feral state to a small animal not much larger than a Shetland pony. On the other hand, the horse was genetically tractable, and breeders learned that hard inbreeding could produce larger, more powerful animals. Still, it was difficult to establish a breed, and only careful control of bloodlines could maintain one. While crossbreeding could produce size and power, it also promoted instability and was best abandoned as soon as the desired traits were "fixed." This was not easy, particularly where the resources available to maintain a nonproductive breeding stock were limited. The net result was that breeds of large, powerful horses suitable for mounted combat were difficult to establish and expensive to maintain, and they were often lost in the turmoil of war. Even when herds were not dispersed or destroyed, a breed could be lost through indiscriminate breeding arising from a need for numbers.

Carisbrooke Castle, on the Isle of Wight, is a motte-and-bailey castle. Note the slope of mounded earth (the motte) on which the castle proper rests. Travel Ink/Gallo Images/Getty Images

THE CASTLE

The great stronghold of medieval Europe, generally the residence of the king or lord of the territory in which it stood, was the castle, which developed rapidly from the 9th century. From rough fortifications that included a high mound encircled by a ditch and surmounted by the leader's particular stronghold, the castle became a complex of stone buildings surrounded and protected by thick stone walls and lines of moats.

THE MOTTE-AND-BAILEY CASTLE

The earliest distinctive European fortification characteristic of feudal patterns of social organization and warfare was the motte-and-bailey castle, which appeared in the 10th and 11th centuries between the Rhine and Loire rivers and eventually spread to most of western Europe. The motte-and-bailey castle consisted of an elevated mound of earth, called the motte, which was crowned with a timber palisade and surrounded by a defensive ditch that also separated the motte from a palisaded outer compound, called the bailey. Access to the motte was by means of an elevated bridge across the ditch from the bailey. The earliest motte-and-bailey castles were built where the ground was suitable and timber available, these factors apparently taking precedence over considerations such as proximity to arable land or trade routes. Later on, as feudal social and economic relationships became more entrenched, castles were sited more for economic, tactical, and strategic advantage and were built of imported stone. The timber palisade was replaced with a keep, or donjon, of dressed stone, and the entire enclosure, called the enceinte, was surrounded by a wall.

The motte-and-bailey castle was not the only pattern of European fortification. There was, for example, a tradition of fortified towns, stemming from Roman fortification, that enjoyed a tenuous existence throughout the Dark Ages, particularly in the Mediterranean world.

STONE FORTIFICATIONS

The greatest weakness of timber fortifications was vulnerability to fire. In addition, a determined attacker, given enough archers to achieve fire dominance over the palisade, could quickly chop his way in. A stone curtain wall, on the other hand, had none of these deficiencies. It could be made high enough to frustrate improvised escalade and, unlike a wooden palisade, could be fitted with a parapet and crenellated firing positions along the top to give cover to defending archers and crossbowmen. Stone required little maintenance or upkeep, and it suffered by comparison with timber only in the high capital investment required to build with it.

Given walls high enough to defeat casual escalade, the prime threats to stone fortresses were the battering ram and attempts to pry chunks out of the wall or undermine it. Since these tactics benefited from an unprotected footing at the base of the wall, most of the refinements of medieval fortress architecture were intended to deny an undisturbed approach. Where terrain permitted, a moat was dug around the enceinte. Towers were made with massive, protruding feet to frustrate attempts at mining. Protruding towers also enabled defenders to bring flanking fire along the face and foot of the wall, and the towers were made higher than the wall to give additional range to archers and crossbowmen. The walls themselves were fitted with provisions for hoardings, which were overhanging wooden galleries from which arrows, stones, and unpleasant substances such as boiling tar and pitch could be dropped or poured on an attacker. Hoardings gave way to machicolations, permanent overhanging galleries of stone that became a distinctive feature of medieval European fortress architecture.

Castle entrances, which were few and small to begin with, were protected by barbicans, low-lying outworks dominated by the walls and towers behind. Gates were generally deeply recessed and backed by a portcullis, a latticework grate suspended in a slot that could be dropped quickly to prevent surprise entry. The gate could also be sealed by means of a drawbridge. These measures were sufficiently effective that medieval sieges were settled more often by treachery, starvation, or disease than by breached walls and undermined towers.

SIEGE WEAPONS

The most basic means of taking a fortress were to storm the gate or go over the wall by simple escalade using ladders, but these methods rarely succeeded except by surprise or treachery. Beginning in the 9th century, European engineers constructed wheeled wooden siege towers, called belfroys. These were fitted with drawbridges, which could be dropped onto the parapet, and with protected firing positions from which the defending parapets could be swept by arrow fire. Constructing one of these towers and moving it forward against an active defense was a considerable feat of engineering and arms. Typically, the moat had to be filled and leveled, all under defensive fire, and attempts to burn or dismount the tower had to be prevented. The wooden towers were vulnerable to fire, so that their faces were generally covered with hides.

Battering rams were capable of bringing down sections of wall, given sufficient time, manpower, and determination.

Large battering rams were mounted on wheels and were covered by a mobile shed for protection from defensive fire.

The most powerful method of direct attack on the structure of a fortress was mining, digging a gallery beneath the walls and supporting the gallery with wooden shoring. Once completed, the mine was fired to burn away the shoring; this collapsed the gallery and brought down the walls. Mining, of course, required suitable ground and was susceptible to countermining by an alert defender.

THE TREBUCHET

In general, the mechanical artillery of medieval times was inferior to that of the Classical world. The one exception was the trebuchet, an engine worked by counterpoise. Counterpoise engines appeared in the 12th century and largely replaced torsion engines by the middle of the 13th. The trebuchet worked something like a seesaw. Suspended from an elevated wooden frame, the arm of the trebuchet pivoted from a point about one-quarter of the way down its length. A large weight, or counterpoise, was suspended from the short end, and the long end was fitted with a hollowed-out spoonlike cavity or a sling. (A sling added substantially to the trebuchet's range.) The long end was winched down, raising the counterpoise; a stone or other missile was put into the spoon or sling, and the arm was released to fly upward, hurling the missile in a high, looping arc toward its

A reconstructed trebuchet, a medieval siege weapon that operated by counterpoise. Danita Delimont/Gallo Images/ Getty Images

target. Though almost anything could be thrown, spherical projectiles of cut stone were the preferred ammunition.

Trebuchets might have a fixed counterpoise, a pivoted counterpoise, or a counterpoise that could be slid up and down the arm to adjust for range. Ropes were frequently attached to the counterpoise to be pulled on for extra power. Modern experiments suggest that a trebuchet with an arm about 15 metres (50 feet) long would have been capable of throwing a 135-kg (300-pound) stone to a distance of 275 metres (300 yards); such a trebuchet would have had a counterpoise of about 10 tons. Though the rate of fire was slow, and prodigious quantities of timber and labour were required to build and serve one, a large trebuchet could do serious damage to stone fortifications. The machines were apparently quite accurate, and small trebuchets were useful in sweeping parapets of archers and crossbowmen.

GREEK FIRE

Greek fire was a weapon that had a decisive tactical and strategic impact in the defense of the Byzantine Empire. It was first used against the Arabs at the siege of Constantinople of 673. Greek fire was a liquid that ignited on contact with seawater. It was viscous and burned fiercely, even in water. Sand and—according to legend—urine were the only effective means of extinguishing the flames. It was expelled by a pumplike device similar to a 19th-century hand-pumped fire engine, and it may also have been thrown from catapults in breakable containers. Although the exact ingredients of Greek fire were a Byzantine state secret, other powers eventually developed and used similar compositions. The original formula was lost and remains unknown. The most likely ingredients were colloidal suspensions of metallic sodium, lithium, or potassium—or perhaps quicklime—in a petroleum base.

Greek fire was particularly effective in naval combat, and it constituted one of the few incendiary weapons of warfare afloat that were used effectively without backfiring on their users. It may have been used following the sack of Constantinople by Venetian-supported crusaders in 1204, but it probably disappeared from use after the fall of Constantinople to the Turks in 1453.

THE HORSE ARCHER

The age of cavalry has come to be viewed from a European perspective, since it was there that infantry was overthrown and there that the greatest and most far-reaching changes occurred. But it was by no means an exclusively European phenomenon; to the contrary, the mounted warrior's tactical supremacy was less complete in western Europe than in any other region of comparably advanced technology save Japan, where a strikingly parallel feudal situation prevailed.

Indeed, from the 1st century CE nomadic horse archers had strengthened their hold over the Eurasian Steppes, the Iranian plateau, and the edges of the Fertile Crescent, and, in a series of waves extending through medieval times, they entered Europe, China, and India and even touched Japan briefly in the 13th century. The most important of these incursions into the European and Chinese military ecospheres left notable marks on the military technology of East Asia and the Byzantine Empire, as well as on the kingdoms of Europe.

THE HUNS AND AVARS

The first of the major horse nomad incursions into Europe were the Hunnish invasions of the 4th century. The Huns' primary significance in the history of military technology was in expanding the use of the composite recurved bow into the eastern Roman Empire. This important instance of technological borrowing constituted one of the few times in which a traditional military skill as physiologically and economically demanding as composite archery was successfully transplanted out of its original cultural context.

The Avars of the 6th and 7th centuries were familiar with the stirrup, and they may have introduced it into Europe. Some of the earliest unequivocal evidence of the use of the stirrup comes from Avar graves.

THE BYZANTINE CATAPHRACT

Although they continued to make effective use of both shock and missile infantry, the Byzantines turned to cavalry earlier and more completely than did the western Roman Empire. After an extended period of dependence on Teutonic and Hunnish mercenary cavalry, the reforms of the emperors Maurice and Heraclius in the 6th and 7th centuries developed an effective provincial militia based on the institution of *pronoia*, the award of nonhereditary grants of land capable of supporting an armoured horse archer called a cataphract. *Pronoia*, which formed the core of the Byzantine army's strength during the period of its greatest efficiency in the 8th through 10th centuries, entailed the adoption of the Hunnish composite recurved bow by native troopers.

The Byzantine cataphract was armed with bow, lance, sword, and dagger. He wore a shirt of mail or scale armour and an iron helm, and carried a small, round, ironbound shield of wood that could be strapped to the forearm or slung from the waist. The foreheads and breasts of officers' horses and those of men in the front rank were protected with frontlets and poitrels of iron. The militia cataphracts were backed by units of similarly armed regulars and mercenary regiments of Teutonic heavy shock cavalry of the imperial guard. Mercenary horse archers from the steppe continued to be used as light cavalry.

THE TURKS

The infiltration of Turkish tribes into the Eurasian military ecosphere was distinguished from earlier steppe nomad invasions in that the raiders were absorbed culturally through Islamization. The long-term results of this wave of nomadic horse archers were profound, leading to the extinction of the Byzantine Empire.

Turkish horse archers, of whom the Seljuqs were representative, were lightly armoured and mounted but extremely mobile. Their armour generally consisted of an iron helmet and, perhaps, a shirt of mail or scale armour (called brigandine). They carried small, light, one-handed shields, usually of wicker fitted with an iron boss. Their principal offensive arms were lance, sabre, and bow. The Turkish bow developed in response to the demands of mounted combat against lightly armoured adversaries on the open steppe; as a consequence, it seems to have had greater range but less penetrative and knockdown power at medium and short ranges than its Byzantine equivalents. Turkish horses, though hardy and agile, were not as large or powerful as Byzantine chargers. Therefore, Turkish horse archers could not stand up to a charge of Byzantine cataphracts, but their greater mobility generally enabled them to stay out of reach and fire arrows from a distance, wearing their adversaries down and killing their horses.

THE MONGOLS

The 13th-century Mongol armies of Genghis Khan and his immediate successors depended on large herds of grass-fed Mongolian ponies, as many as six or eight to a warrior. The ponies were relatively small but agile and hardy, well-adapted to the harsh climate of the steppes. The Mongol warrior's principal weapon was the composite recurved bow, of which he might carry as many as three. Characteristically, each man carried a short bow for use from the saddle and a long bow for use on foot. The former, firing light arrows, was for skirmishing and long-range harassing fire; the latter had the advantage in killing power at medium ranges. The saddle bow was probably capable of sending a light arrow more than 450 metres (500 yards); the heart of the long bow's engagement envelope would have been about 90–320 metres (100–350 yards), close to that of the contemporary English longbow. Each warrior carried several extra quivers of arrows on campaign. He also carried a sabre or scimitar, a lasso, and perhaps a lance. Personal armour included a helmet and breastplate of iron or lacquered leather, though some troops wore shirts of scale or mail.

Mongol armies were proficient at military engineering and made extensive use of Chinese technology, including catapults and incendiary devices. These latter probably included predecessors of gunpowder, of which the Mongols were the likely vehicle of introduction into western Europe.

THE INFANTRY REVOLUTION

The appearance of the crossbow as a serious military implement along the northern rim of the western Mediterranean at about the middle of the 9th century marked a growing divergence between the technology of war in Europe and that of the rest of the world. It was the first of a series of technological and tactical developments that culminated in the rise of infantry elites to a position of tactical dominance. This infantry revolution began when the crossbow spread northward into areas that were peripheral to the economic, cultural, and political core of feudal Europe and where the topography was unfavourable for mounted shock action and the land too poor to support an armoured elite. Within this closed military topography, the crossbow soon proved itself the missile weapon par excellence of positional and guerrilla warfare.

The reasons for the crossbow's success were simple: crossbows were capable of killing the most powerful of mounted warriors, yet they were far cheaper than war-horses and armour and were much easier to master than the skills of equestrian combat. Also, it was far easier to learn to fire a crossbow than a long bow of equivalent power. Serious war bows had significant advantages over the crossbow in range, accuracy, and maximum rate of fire, but crossbowmen could be recruited and trained quickly as adults, while a lifetime of constant practice was required to master the Turkish or Mongol composite bow or the English longbow.

The crossbow directly challenged the mounted elite's dominance of the means of armed violence—a point that the lay and ecclesiastical authorities did not miss. In 1139 the second Lateran Council banned the crossbow under penalty of anathema as a weapon "hateful to God and unfit for Christians," and Emperor Conrad III of Germany (reigned 1138–52) forbade its use in his realms. But the crossbow proved useful in the Crusades against the infidel and, once introduced, could not be eradicated in any event. This produced a grudging acceptance among the European mounted elites, and the crossbow underwent a continuous process of technical development toward greater power that ended only in the 16th century, with the replacement of the crossbow by the harquebus and musket.

An independent, reinforcing, and almost simultaneous development was the appearance of the English longbow as the premier missile weapon of western Europe. The signal victory of an outnumbered English army of longbowmen and dismounted men-at-arms over mounted French chivalry supported by mercenary Genoese crossbowmen at Crécy on Aug. 26, 1346, marked the end of massed cavalry charges by European knights for a century and a half.

THE CROSSBOW

The idea of mounting a bow permanently at right angles across a stock that was fitted with a trough for the arrow, or bolt, and a mechanical trigger to hold the drawn string and release it at will was very old. Crossbows were buried in Chinese graves in the 5th century BCE, and the crossbow was a major factor in Chinese warfare by the 2nd century BCE at the latest. The Greeks used the crossbow principle in the *gastrophetes*, and the Romans knew the crossbow proper as the *manuballista*, though they did not use it extensively. The European crossbow of the Middle Ages differed from all of these in its combination of power and portability.

In Europe, crossbows were progressively developed to penetrate armour of increasing thicknesses. In China, on the other hand, crossbow development emphasized rapidity of fire rather than power; by the 16th century, Chinese artisans were making sophisticated lever-actuated rapid-fire crossbows that carried up to 10 bolts in a self-contained magazine. These, however, were feeble weapons by contemporary European standards and had relatively little penetrating power.

Mechanical cocking aids freed the crossbow from the limitations of simple muscular strength. If the bow could be held in a drawn state by a mechanical trigger, then the bow could be drawn in progressive stages using levers, cranks, and gears or windlass-and-pulley mechanisms, thereby multiplying the user's strength. The power of such a weapon, unlike that of the bow, was thus not limited by the constraints of a single muscular spasm.

The crossbowman, unlike the archer, did not have to be particularly strong or vigorous, and his volume of fire was not as limited by fatigue. Nevertheless, the crossbow had serious tactical deficiencies. First, ordinary crossbows for field operations (as opposed to heavy siege crossbows) were outranged by the bow. This was because crossbow bolts were short and heavy, with a flat base to absorb the initial impact of the string. The flat base and relatively crude leather fins (crossbow bolts were produced in volume and were not as carefully finished as arrows) were aerodynamically inefficient, so that velocity fell off more quickly than that of an arrow. These factors, combined with the inherent lack of precision in the trigger and release mechanism, made the ordinary military crossbow considerably shorter-ranged and less accurate than a serious military bow in the hands of a skilled archer. Also, the advantage of the crossbow's greater power was offset by its elaborate winding mechanisms, which took more time to use. The combination of short range, inaccuracy, and slow rate of fire meant that crossbowmen in the open field were extremely vulnerable to cavalry.

The earliest crossbows had a simple bow of wood alone. However, such bows were not powerful enough for serious military use, and by the 11th century they gave way to composite bows of wood, horn, and sinew. The strength of crossbows increased as knightly armour became more effective, and, by the 13th century, bows were being made of mild steel. (The temper and composition of steel used for crossbows had to be precisely controlled, and the expression "crossbow steel" became an accepted term designating steel of the highest quality.) Because composite and steel crossbows were too powerful to be cocked by the strength of the arms alone, a number of mechanical cocking aids were developed. The first such aid of military significance was a hook suspended from the belt: the crossbowman could step down into a stirrup set in the front of the bow's stock, loop the bowstring

Illustration of a medieval crossbowman, dressed in chain mail and cocking his weapon with the aid of a stirrup. Hulton Archive/Getty Images

over the hook, and by straightening up use the powerful muscles of his back and leg to cock the weapon. The belt hook was inadequate for cocking the steel crossbows required to penetrate plate armour, and by the 14th century military crossbows were being fitted with removable windlasses and rack-and-pinion winding mechanisms called cranequins. Though slow, these devices effectively freed the crossbow from limitations on its strength: draw forces well in excess of 450 kg (1,000 pounds) became common, particularly for large siege crossbows.

THE ENGLISH LONGBOW

The longbow evolved during the 12th century in response to the demands of siege and guerrilla operations in the Welsh Marches, a topographically close and economically marginal area that was in many ways similar to the regions in which the crossbow had evolved three centuries earlier. It became the most effective individual missile weapon of western Europe until well into the age of gunpowder and was the only foot bow since classical times to equal the composite recurved bow in tactical effectiveness and power.

While it was heavily dependent on the strength and competence of its user, the longbow in capable hands was far superior to the ordinary military crossbow in range, rate of fire, and accuracy. Made from a carefully cut and shaped stave of yew or elm, it varied in length, according to the height of the user, from about 1.5–2 metres (5–7 feet). The longbow had a shorter maximum range than the short, stiff composite Turkish or Mongol saddle bows of equivalent draw force, but it could drive a heavy arrow through armour with equal efficiency at medium ranges of 135–270 metres (150–300 yards). Each archer would have carried a few selected light arrows for shooting at extreme ranges and could probably have reached 450 metres (500 yards) with these.

The longbow's weakness was that of every serious military bow: the immense amounts of time and energy needed to master it. Confirmation of the extreme demands placed on the archer was found in the skeletal remains of a bowman who went down with the English ship *Mary Rose*, sunk in Portsmouth Harbour in 1545. The archer (identified as such by a quiver, its leather strap still circling his spine) exhibited skeletal deformations caused by the stresses of archery: the bones of his left forearm showed compression thickening, his upper backbone was twisted radially, and the tips of the first three fingers of his right hand were markedly thickened, plainly the results of a lifetime of drawing a bow of great strength. The longbow was dependent upon the life-style of the English yeomanry, and, as that life-style changed to make archery less remunerative and time for its practice less available, the quality of English archery declined. By the last quarter of the 16th century there were few longbowmen available, and the skill and strength of those who responded to muster was on the whole well below the standards of two centuries earlier. An extended debate in the 1580s between advocates of the longbow and proponents of gunpowder weapons hinged mainly on the small numbers and limited skills of available archers, not around any inherent technical deficiency in the weapon itself.

HALBERD AND PIKE

Another important and enduring discovery was made by the Swiss. At the Battle of Morgarten in 1315, Swiss *eidgenossen*, or "oath brothers," learned that an unarmoured man with a 2-metre (7-foot) halberd could dispatch an armoured man-at-arms. Displaying striking adaptability, they replaced some of their halberds with the pike, a 5.5-metre (18-foot) spear with a small, piercing head. No longer outreached by the knight's lance, and displaying far greater cohesion than any knightly army, the Swiss soon showed that they could defeat armoured men-at-arms, mounted or dismounted, given anything like even numbers. With the creation of the pike square tactical formation, the Swiss provided the model for the modern infantry regiment.

The halberd was the only significant medieval shock weapon without classical antecedents. In its basic form, it consisted of a 1.8-metre (6-foot) shaft of ash or another hardwood, mounted by an ax blade that had a forward point for thrusting and a thin projection on the back for piercing armour or pulling a horseman off balance. The halberd was a specialized weapon for fighting armoured men-at-arms and penetrating knightly armour. With the point of this weapon, a halberdier could fend off a mounted lancer's thrusts and, swinging the cutting edge with the full power of his arms and body, could cleave armour, flesh, and bone. The halberd's power was counterbalanced by the vulnerability of taking a full swing with both arms; once committed, the halberdier was totally dependent upon his comrades for protection. This gave halberd fighting a ferocious all-or-nothing quality and placed a premium on cohesion.

While the halberd could penetrate the best plate armour, allowing infantrymen to inflict heavy casualties on their mounted opponents, the lance's advantage in length meant that men-at-arms could inflict heavy casualties in return. The solution was the pike, a staff, usually of ash, that was twice the length of the halberd and had a small piercing head about 25 cm (10 inches) long. Sound infantry armed with the pike could fend off cavalry with ease, even when outnumbered. As with the halberd, effectiveness of shock action with the pike was heavily dependent upon the cohesion and solidity of the troops wielding it. The pike remained a major factor in European warfare until, late in the 17th century, the bayonet gave missile-armed infantry the ability to repel charging cavalry.

CHAPTER 3

THE GUNPOWDER REVOLUTION

Few inventions have had an impact on human affairs as dramatic and decisive as that of gunpowder. The development of a means of harnessing the energy released by a chemical reaction in order to drive a projectile against a target marked a watershed in the harnessing of energy to human needs. Before gunpowder, weapons were designed around the limits of their users' muscular strength. After gunpowder, they were designed more in response to tactical demand.

Technologically, gunpowder bridged the gap between the medieval and modern eras. By the end of the 19th century, when black powder was supplanted by nitrocellulose-based propellants, steam power had become a mature technology, the scientific revolution was in full swing, and the age of electronics and the internal combustion engine was at hand. The connection between gunpowder and steam power is instructive. Steam power as a practical reality depended on the ability to machine iron cylinders precisely and repetitively to predetermined internal dimensions; the methods for doing this were derived from cannon-boring techniques.

Gunpowder bridged the gap between the old and the new intellectually as well as technologically. Black powder was a product of the alchemist's art, and although alchemy presaged science in believing that physical reality was determined by an unvarying set of natural laws, the alchemist's experimental method was hardly scientific. Gunpowder was a simple mixture combined according to empirical recipes developed without benefit of theoretical knowledge of the underlying processes. The development of gunpowder weapons, however, was the first significant success in rationally and systematically

A 16th-century illustration depicting the many uses of gunpowder, including mortars, cannons, and fireworks. Universal Images Group/Hulton Archive/Getty Images

exploiting an energy source whose power could not be perceived directly with the ordinary senses. As such, early gunpowder technology was an important precursor of modern science.

EARLY GUNPOWDER

Chinese alchemists discovered the recipe for what became known as black powder in the 9th century CE; this was a mixture of finely ground potassium nitrate (also called saltpetre), charcoal, and sulfur in approximate proportions of 75:15:10 by weight. The resultant gray powder behaved differently from anything previously known; it exploded on contact with open flame or a red-hot wire, producing a bright flash, a loud report, dense white smoke, and a sulfurous smell. It also produced considerable quantities of superheated gas, which, if confined in a partially enclosed container, could drive a projectile out of the open end.

The Chinese used the substance in rockets, in pyrotechnic projectors much like Roman candles, in crude cannons, and, according to some sources, in bombs thrown by mechanical artillery. This transpired long before gunpowder was known in the West, but development in China stagnated. The development of black powder as a tactically significant weapon was left to the Europeans, who probably acquired it from the Mongols in the 13th century (though diffusion through the Arab Muslim world is also a possibility).

SERPENTINE POWDER

The earliest gunpowder was made by grinding the ingredients separately and mixing them together dry. This was known as serpentine. The behaviour of serpentine was highly variable, depending on a number of factors that were difficult to predict and control. If packed too tightly and not confined, a charge of serpentine might fizzle; conversely, it might develop internal cracks and detonate. When subjected to vibration, as when being transported by wagon, the components of serpentine separated into layers according to relative density, the sulfur settling to the bottom and the charcoal rising to the top. Remixing at the battery was necessary to maintain the proper proportions—an inconvenient and hazardous procedure producing clouds of noxious and potentially explosive dust.

CORNED POWDER

Shortly after 1400, smiths learned to combine the ingredients of gunpowder in water and grind them together as a slurry. This was a significant improvement in several respects. Wet incorporation was more complete and uniform than dry mixing, the process "froze" the components permanently into a stable grain matrix so that separation was no longer a problem, and wet slurry could be ground in large quantities by water-driven mills with little danger of explosion. The use of waterpower also sharply reduced cost.

GUNPOWDER RECIPES

Black powder differed from modern propellants and explosives in a number of important particulars. First, only some 44 percent by weight of a properly burned charge of black powder was converted into propellant gases, the balance being solid residues. The high molecular weights of these residues limited the muzzle velocities of black-powder ordnance to about 600 metres (2,000 feet) per second. Second, unlike modern nitrocellulose-based propellants, the burning rate of black powder did not vary significantly with pressure or temperature. This occurred because the reaction in an exploding charge of black powder was transmitted from grain to grain at a rate some 150 times greater than the rate at which the individual grains were consumed and because black powder burned in a complex series of parallel and mutually dependent exothermal (heat-producing) and endothermal (heat-absorbing) reactions that balanced each other out. The result was an essentially constant burning rate that differed only with the grain size of the powder; the larger the grains, the less surface area exposed to combustion and the slower the rate at which propellant gases were produced.

Nineteenth-century experiments on various black powder recipes revealed sharp differences in the amount of gas produced by charcoal obtained from different kinds of wood. For example, dogwood charcoal decomposed with potassium nitrate was found to yield nearly 25 percent more gas per unit weight than fir, chestnut, or hazel charcoal and some 17 percent more than willow charcoal. These scientific observations confirmed the insistence of early—and thoroughly unscientific—texts that charcoal from different kinds of wood was suited to different applications. Willow charcoal, for example, was preferred for cannon powder and dogwood charcoal for small arms—a preference substantiated by 19th-century tests. In addition, a preference for urine instead of water as the incorporation agent might have had some basis in fact because urine is rich in nitrates; so might the view that a beer drinker's urine was preferable to that of an abstemious person and a wine drinker's urine best of all.

For all this, the empirically derived recipe for gunpowder was fixed during the 14th century and hardly varied thereafter. Subsequent improvements were almost entirely concerned with the manufacturing process and with the ability to purify and control the quality of the ingredients.

After grinding, the slurry was dried in a sheet or cake. It was then processed in stamping mills, which typically used hydraulically tripped wooden hammers to break the sheet into grains. After being tumbled to wear the sharp edges off the grains and impart a glaze to their surface, they were sieved. The grain size varied from coarse—about the size of grains of wheat or corn (hence the name corned powder)—to extremely fine. Powder too fine to be used was reincorporated into the slurry for reprocessing. Corned powder burned more uniformly and rapidly than serpentine. The result was a stronger powder that rendered many older guns dangerous.

REFINEMENTS IN BALLISTICS

Late medieval and early modern gunners preferred large-grained powder for cannons, medium-grained powder for shoulder arms, and fine-grained powder for pistols and priming—and they were correct in their preferences. In cannons, the slower burning rate of large-grained powder allowed a relatively massive, slowly accelerating projectile to begin moving as the pressure built gradually, reducing peak pressure and putting less stress on the gun. The fast burning rate of fine-grained powders, on the other hand, permitted internal pressure to peak before the light, rapidly accelerating projectile of a small arm had exited the muzzle. But the early modern gunner had no provable rationale for his preferences, and in the 18th century European armies standardized on fine-grained musket powder for cannons as well as small arms.

Then, beginning in the late 18th century, the application of science to ballistics began to produce practical results. The ballistic pendulum, invented by the English mathematician Benjamin Robins, provided a means of measuring muzzle velocity and, hence, of accurately gauging the effective power of a given quantity of powder. A projectile was fired horizontally into the pendulum's bob (block of wood), which absorbed the projectile's momentum and converted it into upward movement. Momentum is the product of mass and velocity, and the law of conservation of momentum dictates that the total momentum of a system is conserved, or remains constant. Thus the projectile's velocity, v, may be determined from the equation $mv = (m + M)V$, which gives

$$v = \frac{m + M}{m}V,$$

where m is the mass of the projectile, M is the mass of the bob, and V is the velocity of the bob and embedded projectile after impact.

The initial impact of science on internal ballistics was to show that traditional powder charges for cannons were much larger than necessary. Refinements in the manufacture of gunpowder followed. About 1800 the British introduced cylinder-burned charcoal—that is, charcoal burned in enclosed vessels rather than in pits. With this method, wood was converted to charcoal at a uniform and precisely controlled temperature. The result was greater uniformity and, since fewer of the volatile trace elements were burned off, more powerful powder. Later, powder for very large ordnance was made from charcoal that was deliberately "overburned" to reduce the initial burning rate and, hence, the stress on the gun.

Beginning in the mid-19th century, the use of extremely large guns for naval warfare and coastal defense pressed existing materials and methods of cannon construction to the limit. This led to the development of methods for measuring pressures within the gun, which involved cylindrical punches mounted in holes drilled at right angles through the barrel. The pressure of the propellant gases forced the punches outward against soft copper plates, and the maximum pressure was then determined by calculating the amount of pressure needed to create an indentation of equal depth in the copper. The ability to measure pressures within a gun led to the design of cannons made thickest where internal pressures were greatest—that is, near the breech. The resultant "soda bottle" cannon of the mid- to late 19th century, which had fat breeches curving down to short, slim muzzles, bore a strange resemblance to the very earliest European gun of which a depiction survives, that of the Walter de Millimete manuscript of 1327.

THE DEVELOPMENT OF ARTILLERY

The earliest known gunpowder weapons vaguely resembled an old-fashioned soda bottle or a deep-throated mortar and pestle. The earliest such weapon, depicted in the English de Millimete manuscript, was about a metre (3.3 feet) long with a bore diameter of about 5 cm (2 inches). The projectile resembled an arrow with a wrapping around the shaft, probably of leather, to provide a gas seal within the bore. Firing was apparently accomplished by applying a red-hot wire to a touchhole drilled through the top of the thickest part of the breech. The gun was laid horizontally on a trestle table without provision for adjusting elevation or absorbing recoil—a tribute to its modest power, which would have been only marginally greater than that of a large crossbow.

The breakthrough that led to the emergence of true cannons derived from three basic perceptions. The first was that gunpowder's propellant force could be used most effectively by confining it within a tubular barrel. This stemmed from an awareness that gunpowder's explosive energy did not act instantaneously upon the projectile but had to develop its force across time and space. The second perception was that methods of construction derived from cooperage could be used to construct tubular wrought-iron gun barrels. The third perception was that a spherical ball was the optimal projectile. The result was modern artillery.

WROUGHT-IRON MUZZLE-LOADERS

The earliest guns were probably cast from brass or bronze. Bell-founding techniques would have sufficed to produce the desired shapes, but alloys of copper, tin, and zinc were expensive and, at first, not well adapted to the containment of high-temperature, high-velocity gases. Wrought iron solved both of these problems. Construction involved forming a number of longitudinal staves into a tube by beating them around a form called a mandrel and welding them together. (Alternatively, a single sheet of iron could be wrapped around the mandrel and then welded closed; this was particularly suitable for smaller pieces.) The tube was then reinforced with a number of rings or sleeves (in effect, hoops). These were forged with an inside diameter about the same as the outside of the tube, raised to red or white heat, and slid into place over the cooled tube, where they were held firmly in place by thermal contraction. The sleeves or rings were butted against one another and the gaps between them sealed by a second layer of hoops. Forging a strong, gastight breech presented a particular problem that was usually solved by welding a tapered breech plug between the staves.

Hoop-and-stave construction permitted the fabrication of guns far larger than had been made previously. By the last quarter of the 14th century, wrought-iron siege bombards were firing stone cannonballs of 200 kg (450 pounds) and more. These weapons were feasible only with projectiles of stone. Cast iron has more than two and a half times the density of marble or granite, and gunners quickly learned that a cast-iron cannonball with a charge of good corned powder behind it was unsafe in any gun large enough for serious siege work.

WROUGHT-IRON BREECHLOADERS

Partly because of the difficulties of making a long, continuous barrel, and partly because of the relative ease of loading a powder charge into a short breechblock, gunsmiths soon learned to make cannons in which the barrel and powder chamber were separate. Since the charge and projectile were loaded into the rear of the barrel, these were called breechloaders. The breechblock was mated to the barrel by means of a recessed lip at the chamber mouth. Before firing, it was dropped into the stock and forced forward against the barrel by hammering a wedge into place behind it; after the weapon was fired, the wedge was knocked out and the block was removed for reloading. This scheme had significant advantages, particularly in the smaller classes of naval swivel guns and fortress wallpieces, where the use of multiple breechblocks permitted a high rate of fire. Small breechloaders continued to be used in these ways well into the 17th century.

The essential deficiency of early breechloaders was the imperfect gas seal between breechblock and barrel, a problem that was not solved until the advent of the brass cartridge late in the 19th century. Hand-forging techniques could not produce a truly gastight seal, and combustion gases escaping through the inevitable crevices eroded the metal, causing safety problems. Wrought-iron cannons must have required constant maintenance and care, particularly in a saltwater environment.

A drawing of the wrought-iron breech-loading gun and carriage from the English warship Mary Rose, *which sank in 1545.* SSPL via Getty Images

Wrought-iron breechloaders were the first cannons to be produced in significant numbers. Their tactical viability was closely linked to the economics of cannonballs of cut stone, which, modern preconceptions to the contrary, were superior to cast-iron projectiles in many respects. Muzzle velocities of black-powder weapons were low, and smoothbore cannons were inherently inaccurate, so that denser projectiles of iron had no advantage in effective range.

Cannons designed to fire a stone projectile were considerably lighter than those designed to fire an iron ball of the same weight; as a result, stone-throwing cannons were for many years cheaper. Also, because stone cannonballs were larger than iron ones of the same weight, they left larger holes after penetrating the target. The principal deficiency of stone-throwing cannons was the enormous amount of skilled labour required to cut a sphere of stone accurately to a predetermined diameter. The acceleration of the wage–price spiral in the 15th and 16th centuries made stone-throwing cannons obsolete in Europe.

CAST BRONZE MUZZLE-LOADERS

The advantages of cast bronze for constructing large and irregularly shaped objects of a single piece were well understood from sculpture and bell founding, but a number of problems had to be overcome before the material's plasticity could be applied to ordnance. Most important, alloys had to be developed that were strong enough to withstand the shock and internal pressures of firing without being too brittle. This was not simply a matter of finding the optimal proportions of copper and tin; bronze alloys used in cannon founding were prone to internal cavities and "sponginess," and foundry practices had to be developed to overcome the inherent deficiencies of the metal. The essential technical problems were solved by the first decades of the 15th century, and, by the 1420s and '30s, European cannon founders were casting bronze pieces that rivaled the largest of the wrought-iron bombards in size.

Developments in foundry practice were accompanied by improvements in weapon design. Most notable was the practice of casting cylindrical mounting lugs, called trunnions, integral with the barrel. Set just forward of the centre of gravity, trunnions provided the principal point for attaching the barrel to the carriage and a pivot for adjusting the vertical angle of the gun. This permitted the barrel to be adjusted in elevation by sliding a wedge, or quoin, beneath the breech. At first, trunnions were supplemented by lifting lugs cast atop the barrel at the centre of gravity. By the 16th century most European founders were casting these lugs in the shape of leaping dolphins, and a similarly shaped fixture was often cast on the breech of the gun.

Toward the end of the 15th century, French founders combined these features with efficient gun carriages for land use. French carriage design involved suspending the barrel from its trunnions between a pair of heavy wooden side pieces; an axle and two large wheels were then mounted forward of the trunnions, and the rear of the side pieces descended to the ground to serve as a trail. The trail was left on the ground during firing and absorbed the recoil of the gun, partly through sliding friction and partly by digging into the ground. Most important, the gun could be transported without dismounting the barrel by lifting the trail onto the limber, a two-wheeled mount that served as a pivoting front axle and point of attachment for the team of horses. This improved carriage, though heavy in its proportions, would have been familiar to a gunner of Napoleonic times. Sometime before the middle of the 16th century, English smiths developed a highly compact four-wheeled truck carriage for mounting trunnion-equipped shipboard ordnance, resulting in cannons that would have been familiar to a naval gunner of Horatio Nelson's day in the early 19th century.

By the early 1500s, cannon founders throughout Europe had learned to manufacture good ordnance of cast bronze. Cannons were cast in molds of vitrified clay, suspended vertically in a pit. Normally, they were cast breech down; this placed the molten metal at the breech under pressure, resulting in a denser and stronger alloy around the chamber, the most critical point. Subsequent changes in foundry practice were incremental and took effect gradually. As founders established mastery over bronze, cannons became shorter and lighter. In about 1750, advances in boring machines and cutting tools made it possible for advanced foundries to cast barrels as solid blanks and then bore them out. Until then cannons were cast hollow—that is, the bore was cast around a core suspended in the mold. Ensuring that the bore was precisely centred was a particularly critical part of the casting process, and small wrought-iron fixtures called chaplets were used to hold the core precisely in place. These were cast into the bronze and remained a part of the gun. Boring produced more accurate weapons and improved the quality of the bronze, since impurities in the molten metal, which gravitate toward the centre of the mold during solidification, were removed by the boring.

While these changes were important operationally, they represented only marginal improvements to the same basic technology. A first-class bronze cannon of 1500 differed hardly at all in essential technology and ballistic performance from a cannon of 1850 designed to shoot a ball of the same weight. The modern gun would have been shorter and lighter, and it would have been mounted on a more efficient carriage, but it would have fired its ball no farther and no more accurately.

CAST-IRON CANNONS

In 1543 an English parson, working on a royal commission from Henry VIII, perfected a method for casting reasonably safe, operationally efficient cannons of iron. The nature of the breakthrough in production technology is unclear, but it probably involved larger furnaces and a more efficient organization of resources.

Cast-iron cannons were significantly heavier and bulkier than bronze guns firing the same weight of ball. Unlike bronze cannons, they were prone to internal corrosion. Moreover, when they failed, they did not tear and rupture like bronze guns but burst into fragments like a bomb. They possessed, however, the overwhelming advantage of costing only about one-third as much. This gave the English, who alone mastered the process until well into the 17th century, a significant commercial advantage by enabling them to arm large numbers of ships. The Mediterranean nations were unable to cast significant quantities of iron artillery until well into the 19th century.

The smaller size and low cost of cast-iron cannons, one of which is shown stationed at a ship's porthole, allowed the British Royal Navy to arm many of its vessels. SSPL via Getty Images

EARLY USE OF ARTILLERY

Early gunpowder artillery was known by a bewildering variety of names. (The word *cannon* became dominant only gradually, and the modern use of the term to describe a gun large enough to fire an explosive shell did not emerge until the 20th century.) The earliest efficient wrought-iron cannons were called *bombards* or *lombards*, a term that continued in use well into the 16th century. The term *basilisk*, the name of a mythical dragonlike beast of withering gaze and flaming breath, was applied to early "long" cannons capable of firing cast-iron projectiles. Early cannon terminology being anything but consistent, however, any particularly large and powerful cannon might be called a basilisk.

Founders had early adopted the practice of classifying cannons by the weight of the ball, so that, for example, a 12-pounder fired a 5.4-kg (12-pound) cannonball. By the 16th century, gunners had adopted the custom of describing the length of a cannon's bore in calibres, that is, in multiples of the bore diameter. These became basic tools of classification and remained so into the modern era with certain categories of ordnance such as large naval guns. Also by the 16th century, European usage had divided ordnance into three categories according to bore length and the type of projectile fired. The first category was the culverins, "long" guns with bores on the order of 30 calibres or more. The second was the cannons, or cannons-of-battery, named for their primary function of battering down fortress walls; these typically had barrels of 20 to 25 calibres. The third category of ordnance was the pedreros, stone-throwing guns with barrels of as little as eight to 10 calibres that were used in siege and naval warfare.

Mortars were a separate type of ordnance. With very wide bores of even fewer calibres than those of the pedreros, they were used in siege warfare for lobbing balls at a very high trajectory (over 45°). Mortars owed their name to the powder chamber of reduced diameter that was recessed into the breech; this made them similar in appearance to the mortars used to pulverize grain and chemicals by hand. Unlike the longer cannon, mortars were cast with trunnions at the breech and were elevated by placing wedges beneath the muzzle.

SPECIAL-PURPOSE SHOT

Both culverins and cannons-of-battery generally fired cast-iron balls. When fired against masonry walls, heavy iron balls tended to pulverize stone and brick. Large stone cannonballs, on the other hand, were valued for the shock of their impact, which could bring down large pieces of wall. Undercutting the bottom of a wall with iron cannonballs, then using the heavy impact of large stone shot to bring it down, was a standard tactic of siege warfare. (Ottoman gunners were particularly noted for this approach.)

In the 15th century exploding shot was developed by filling hollow cast-iron balls with gunpowder and fitting a fuze that had to be lit just before firing. These ancestors of the modern exploding shell were extremely dangerous to handle, as they were known to explode prematurely or, with equally catastrophic results, jam in the gun barrel. For this reason they were used only in the short-bored mortars.

For incendiary purposes, iron balls were heated red-hot in a fire before loading. (In that case, moist clay was sometimes packed atop the wadding that separated the ball from the powder charge.) Other projectiles developed for special purposes included the carcass, canister, grapeshot, chain shot, and bar shot. The carcass was a thin-walled shell containing incendiary materials. Rounds of canister and grapeshot consisted of numerous small missiles, usually iron or lead balls, held together in various ways for simultaneous loading into the gun but designed to separate upon leaving the muzzle. Because they dispersed widely upon leaving the gun, the projectiles were especially effective at short range against massed troops. Bar shot and chain shot consisted of two heavy projectiles joined by a bar or a chain. Whirling in their trajectories, they were especially effective at sea in cutting the spars and rigging of sailing vessels.

Gunnery

During most of the black-powder era, with smoothbore cannons firing spherical projectiles, artillery fire was never precisely accurate at long ranges. (Aiming and firing were particularly difficult in naval gunnery, since the gunner had to predict the roll of the ship in order to hit the target.) Gunners aimed by sighting along the top of the barrel, or "by the line of metals," then stepped away before firing to avoid the recoil. The basic relationship between range and elevation being understood, some accuracy was introduced through the use of the gunner's quadrant, in which the angle of elevation of a gun barrel was measured by inserting one leg of the quadrant into the barrel and reading the angle marked on the scale by a vertically hanging plumb line.

Nevertheless, the inherent inaccuracy of smoothbore artillery meant that most shooting was done at short ranges of 900 metres (1,000 yards) or less. At these ranges, estimating elevation by rule of thumb was sufficient. For attacking fortress walls, early modern gunners preferred a range of 55 to 75 metres (60 to 80 yards); a range of 90 to 135 metres (100 to 150 yards) was acceptable, but 270 metres (300 yards) or more was considered excessive.

The First Small Arms

Small arms did not exist as a distinct class of gunpowder weapon until the middle of the 15th century. Until then, hand cannons differed from their larger relatives only in size. They looked much the same, consisting of a barrel fastened to a simple wooden stock that was braced beneath the gunner's arm. A second person was required to fire the weapon. About the middle of the 15th century, a series of connected developments established small arms as an important and distinct category of weaponry. The first of these was the development of slow match—or match, as it was commonly called. This was cord or twine soaked in a solution of potassium nitrate and dried. When lit, match smoldered at the end in a slow, controlled manner. Slow match found immediate acceptance among artillerists and remained a standard part of the gunner's kit for the next four centuries.

The Matchlock

Small arms appeared during the period 1460–80 with the development of mechanisms that applied match to hand-portable weapons. German gunsmiths apparently led the way. The first step was a simple S-shaped "trigger," called a serpentine, fastened to the side of a hand cannon's stock. The serpentine was pivoted in the middle and had a set of adjustable jaws, or dogs, on the upper end that held the smoldering end of a length of match. Pulling up on the bottom of the serpentine brought the tip of the match down into contact with powder in the flashpan, a small, saucer-shaped depression surrounding the touchhole atop the barrel. This arrangement made it possible for one gunner to aim and fire, and it was quickly improved on. The first and most basic change was the migration of the touchhole to the right side of the barrel, where it was served by a flashpan equipped with a hinged or pivoting cover that protected the priming powder from wind, rain, and rough handling. The serpentine was replaced by a mechanism, enclosed within the gunstock, that consisted of a trigger, an arm holding the match with its adjustable jaws at the end, a sear connecting trigger and arm, and a mechanical linkage opening the flashpan cover as the match descended. These constituted the matchlock, and they made possible modern small arms.

One final refinement was a spring that drove the arm holding the match downward into the pan when released by the sear. This mechanism, called the snap matchlock, was the forerunner of the flintlock. The fabrication of these devices fell to locksmiths, the only sizable body of craftsmen accustomed to constructing metal mechanisms with the necessary ruggedness and precision. They gave to the firing mechanism the enduring name lock.

The development of mechanical locks was accompanied by the evolution of gunstocks with proper grips and an enlarged butt to transmit the recoil to the user's body. The result was the matchlock harquebus, the dominant military small arm of the 15th century and the direct ancestor of the modern musket. The harquebus was at first butted to the breastbone, but, as the power of firearms increased, the advantages of absorbing the recoil on the shoulder came to be appreciated. The matchlock harquebus changed very little in its essentials until it was replaced by the flintlock musket in the final years of the 17th century.

THE WHEEL LOCK

The principal difficulty with the matchlock mechanism was the need to keep a length of match constantly smoldering. German gunsmiths addressed themselves to this problem early in the 16th century. The result was the wheel lock mechanism, consisting of a serrated wheel rotated by a spring and a spring-loaded set of jaws that held a piece of iron pyrites against the wheel. Pulling the trigger caused the wheel to rotate, directing a shower of sparks into the flashpan. The wheel lock firearm could be carried in a holster and kept ready to fire indefinitely, but, being delicate and expensive, it did not spread beyond cavalry elites and had a limited impact on warfare as a whole.

THE FLINTLOCK

Flintlock firing mechanisms were known by the middle of the 16th century, about a hundred years before they made their appearance in quantity in infantry muskets. A flintlock was similar to a wheel lock except that ignition came from a blow of flint against steel, with the sparks directed into the priming powder in the pan. This lock was an adaptation of the tinderbox used for starting fires.

In the several different types of flintlocks that were produced, the flint was always held in a small vise, called a cock, which described an arc around its pivot to strike the steel (generally called the frizzen) a glancing blow. A spring inside the lock was connected through a tumbler to the cock. The sear, a small piece of metal attached to the trigger, either engaged the tumbler inside the lock or protruded through the lock plate to make direct contact with the cock.

Flintlocks were not as surefire as either the matchlock or the wheel lock, but they were cheaper than the latter, contained fewer delicate parts, and were not as difficult to repair in primitive surroundings. In common with the wheel locks they had the priceless advantage of being ready to fire immediately. A flintlock small arm was slightly faster to load than a matchlock, if the flint itself did not require adjustment.

CHAPTER 4

FORTIFICATION AND MODERN BODY ARMOUR

Fortification is any work erected to strengthen a position against attack. Fortifications are usually of two types: permanent and field. Permanent fortifications include elaborate forts and troop shelters and are most often erected in times of peace or upon threat of war. Field fortifications, which are constructed when in contact with an enemy or when contact is imminent, consist of entrenched positions for personnel and crew-served weapons, cleared fields of fire, and obstacles such as explosive mines, barbed-wire entanglements, felled trees, and antitank ditches.

Both field and permanent fortifications often take advantage of natural obstacles, such as canals and rivers, and they are usually camouflaged or otherwise concealed. Both types are designed to assist the defender to obtain the greatest advantage from his own strength and weapons while preventing the enemy from using his resources to best advantage.

In addition to seeking protection behind works, soldiers often wear protective clothing that has at least some ability to deflect or absorb the impact of projectiles or other weapons that may be used against its wearer. Until modern times, armour worn by combatants in warfare was laboriously fashioned and frequently elaborately wrought, reflecting the personal importance placed by the vulnerable soldier on its protection and also frequently the social importance of its wearer within the group. Modern technology has brought about the development of lighter protective materials that are fashioned into a variety of apparel suited to the hazards of modern warfare. With the rise of terrorism and the use of powerful personal weapons by criminals, armour is now frequently worn by police, by private nonmilitary security forces, and even by noncombatants who might be targets of attack.

FORTIFICATION

Before gunpowder artillery, a well-maintained stone castle, secured against escalade by high curtain walls and flanking towers, provided almost unbreachable security against attack. Artillery at first did little to change this. Large wrought-iron cannon capable of throwing wall-smashing balls of cut stone appeared toward the end of the 14th century, but they were neither efficient nor mobile. Indeed, the size and unwieldiness of early firearms and cannon suited them more for fortress arsenals than for the field, and adjustments to gunpowder by fortification engineers quickly tilted the balance of siege operations toward the defense. Gunports were cut low in walls for covering ditches with raking fire, reinforced platforms and towers were built to withstand the recoil shock of defensive cannon, and the special firing embrasures for crossbows were modified into gunports for hand cannon, with sophisticated vents to carry away the smoke. The name of the first truly effective small arm, the *hackenbüsche*, or hackbutt, is telling. The weapon took its name, literally "hook gun," from a projection welded beneath the forward barrel that was hooked over the edge of a parapet in order to absorb the piece's recoil.

THE EFFECT OF ARTILLERY AND SIEGECRAFT ON FORTIFICATION DESIGN

The inviolability of the medieval curtain wall came to an end in the 15th century, with the development of effective cast-bronze siege cannon. Many of the basic technical developments that led to the perfection of heavy bronze ordnance were pioneered by German founders. Frederick I, elector of Brandenburg from 1417 to 1425, used cannon systematically to defeat the castles of his rivals one by one in perhaps the earliest politically decisive application of gunpowder technology. The French and Ottomans were the first to bring siege artillery to bear in a decisive manner outside their own immediate regions. Charles VII of France (reigned 1422–61) used siege artillery to reduce English forts in the last stages of the Hundred Years' War. When his grandson Charles VIII invaded Italy in 1494, the impact of technically superior French artillery was immediate and dramatic; the French breached in eight hours the key frontier fortress of Monte San Giovanni, which had previously withstood a siege of seven years.

The impact of Ottoman siege artillery was equally dramatic. Sultan Mehmed II breached the walls of Constantinople in 1453 by means of large bombards, bringing the Byzantine Empire to an end and laying the foundations of Ottoman power. The Turks retained their superiority in siegecraft for another generation, leveling the major Venetian fortifications in southern Greece in 1499–1500 and marching unhindered through the Balkans before being repulsed before Vienna in 1529.

The shock of the sudden vulnerability of medieval curtain walls to French, Ottoman, and, to a lesser extent, German siege cannon quickly gave way to attempts by military engineers to redress the balance. At first, these consisted of the obvious and expensive expedients of counter-battery fire. By the 1470s, towers were being cut down to the height of the adjacent wall, and firing platforms of packed earth were built behind walls and in the lower stories of towers. Italian fortress architects experimented with specially designed artillery towers with low-set gunports sited to sweep the fortress ditch with fire; some were even sited to cover adjacent sections of wall with flanking fire. However, most of these fortresses still had high, vertical walls and were therefore vulnerable to battery.

A definitive break with the medieval past was marked by two Italian sieges. The first of these was the defense of Pisa in 1500 against a combined Florentine and French army. Finding their wall crumbling to French cannon fire, the Pisans in desperation constructed an earthen rampart behind the threatened sector. To their surprise and relief, they discovered not only that the sloping earthen rampart could be defended against escalade but that it was far more resistant to cannon shot than the vertical stone wall that it supplanted. The second siege was that of Padua in 1509. Entrusted with the defense of this Venetian city, a monk-engineer named Fra Giocondo cut down the city's medieval wall. He then surrounded the city with a broad ditch that could be swept by flanking fire from gunports set low in projections extending into the ditch. Finding that their cannon fire made little impression on these low ramparts, the French and allied besiegers made several bloody and fruitless assaults and then withdrew.

THE SUNKEN PROFILE

While Pisa demonstrated the strength of earthen ramparts, Padua showed the power of a sunken profile supported by flanking fire in the ditch. With these two cities pointing the way, basic changes were undertaken in fortress design. Fortress walls, still essential for protection against escalade, were dropped into the ground behind a ditch and protected from battery by gradually sloping earthen ramparts beyond. A further refinement was the sloping of the glacis, or forward face of the ramparts, in such a manner that it could be swept by cannon and harquebus fire from the parapet behind the ditch. As a practical matter the scarp, or main fortress wall, now protected from artillery fire by the glacis, was faced with brick or stone for ease of maintenance; the facing wall on the forward side of the ditch, called the counterscarp, was similarly faced. Next, a level, sunken space behind the glacis, the covered way, was provided so that defenders could assemble for a sortie under cover and out of sight of the attackers. This, and the provision of firing embrasures for cannon in the parapet wall, completed the basics of the new fortress profile.

Refinements of the basic sunken design included a palisade of sharpened wooden stakes either in the ditch or immediately behind the glacis and a sunken, level path behind the parapet

for ammunition carts, artillery reinforcements, and relief troops. As attacking and defending batteries became larger, fortress designers placed greater emphasis on outworks intended to push the besieging batteries farther back and out of range.

The profile of the outworks was designed according to the same basic principles applied to the fortress. Well established by 1520, these principles remained essentially unchanged until rifled artillery transformed positional warfare in the mid-19th century.

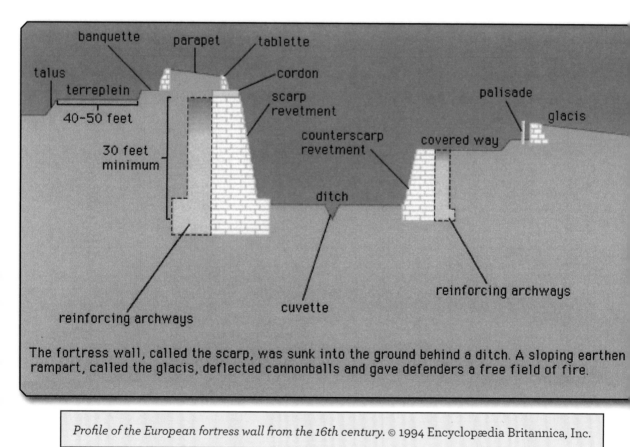

The fortress wall, called the scarp, was sunk into the ground behind a ditch. A sloping earthen rampart, called the glacis, deflected cannonballs and gave defenders a free field of fire.

Profile of the European fortress wall from the 16th century. © 1994 Encyclopædia Britannica, Inc.

THE BASTIONED TRACE

The sunken profile was only half the story of early modern fortress design; the other half was the trace, the outline of the fortress as viewed from above. The new science of trace design was based, in its early stages, on the bastion, a projection from the main fortress wall from which defending fire could sweep the face of adjacent bastions and the wall between. Actually, bastions had been introduced before engineers were fully aware of the power of artillery, so that some early 16th-century Italian fortifications combined sophisticated bastioned traces with outmoded high walls, a shallow ditch, and little or no protective glacis. After early experimentation with rounded contours, which were believed to be stronger, designers came to appreciate the advantages of bastions with polygonal shapes, which eliminated the dead space at the foot of circular towers and provided uninterrupted fields of view and fire. Another benefit of the polygonal bastion's long, straight sections of wall was that larger defensive batteries could be mounted along the parapets.

The relatively simple traces of the early Italian bastioned fortresses proved vulnerable to the ever larger armies and ever more powerful siege trains of the 16th century. In response, outworks were developed, such as ravelins (detached outworks in front of the bastions) and demilunes (semidetached outworks in the ditch between bastions), to shield the main fortress walls from direct battery. The increasing scale of warfare and the greater resources available to the besieger accelerated this development, and systems of outworks grew more and more elaborate and sprawling as a means of slowing the attacker's progress and making it more costly.

By the late 17th century, fortress profiles and traces were closely integrated with one another and with the ground on which they stood. The sophistication of their designs is frequently linked with the name of the French military engineer Sébastien Le Prestre de Vauban.

DURATION OF EARLY MODERN FORTIFICATION

With various refinements, the early modern fortress, based on a combination of the sunken profile and bastioned trace, remained the basic form of permanent fortification until the American Civil War, which saw the first extensive use of heavy rifled cannon made of high-quality cast iron. These guns not only had several times the effective range and accuracy of their predecessors, but they were also capable of firing explosive shells. They did to the early modern fortress what cast-bronze cannon had done to the medieval curtain wall. In 1862 the reduction by rifled Union artillery of Fort Pulaski, a supposedly impregnable Confederate fortification defending Savannah, Ga., marked the beginning of a new chapter in the design of permanent fortifications.

TRENCH WARFARE, 1850–1918

In the American Civil War, field fortifications emerged as an essential of warfare, with both armies employing entrenchments to an extent never before seen. Troops learned to fortify newly won positions immediately; employing spades and axes carried in their packs, they first dug rifle pits and then expanded them into trenches. Early in the war, General Robert E. Lee adopted the frontier rifleman's breastwork composed of two logs on the parapet of the entrenchment, and many of Lee's victories were the result of his ability to use hasty entrenchments as a base for aggressive employment of fire and maneuver. Two notable sieges, that of Vicksburg, Miss., in the west, and Petersburg, Va., in the east, were characterized by the construction of extensive and continuous trench lines that foreshadowed those of World War I. In the Cold Harbor, Va., campaign, when General Ulysses S. Grant sent his troops against Confederate earthworks, he lost 14,000 men in 13 days. Field mines and booby traps were used extensively, and trench mortars were developed to lob shells into opposing trenches.

The lesson taught by accurate, long-range fire from entrenched positions in the American Civil War was lost on European commanders. Even the bitter experiences of appalling losses in the Crimean, Franco-German, and South African (Boer) wars failed to lessen an ardour for the theory of the offensive that was so fervent as to leave little concern for defensive tactics in the field. Few took notice of the immense casualties the Turks inflicted from behind field fortifications in the Russo-Turkish War of 1877–78, and even though the Russo-Japanese War soon after the turn of the century underscored the lethal power of the machine gun and breech-loading rifled artillery, most European commanders saw the increased firepower as more a boon to the offensive than to the defensive.

The fallacy of the faith in offensive firepower was soon convincingly demonstrated in World War I. Once the French had checked the German right wing at the Marne River, the fighting degenerated into what was in effect a massive siege. For 1,000 km (600 miles), from Switzerland to the North Sea, the landscape was soon scarred with opposing systems of zigzag, timber-revetted, sandbag-reinforced trenches, fronted by tangles of barbed wire sometimes more than 45 metres (150 feet) deep and featured here and there by covered dugouts providing shelter for troops and horses and by observation posts in log bunkers or concrete turrets. The trench systems consisted of several lines in depth, so that if the first line was penetrated, the assailants were little better off. Rail and motor transport could rush fresh reserves forward to seal off a gap faster than the attackers could continue forward. Out beyond the trenches and the barbed wire was a muddy, virtually

THE SIEGE OF PETERSBURG

During the American Civil War, Petersburg, Va., an important rail centre 37 km (23 miles) south of Richmond, was a strategic point for the defense of the Confederate capital. In June 1864 the Union army began a siege of both cities, with both sides rapidly constructing fortifications 55 km (35 miles) long. In a series of battles that summer, Union losses were heavy, but, by the end of August, General Ulysses S. Grant had crossed the Petersburg–Weldon Railroad; he captured Fort Harrison on September 29.

By year's end, General Robert E. Lee still held Richmond and Petersburg. However, mostly owing to mismanagement and inefficiency, Southern railroads had broken down or been destroyed. The Confederates were ill-fed to the point of physical exhaustion, and the lack of draft animals and cavalry mounts nearly immobilized the troops. Hunger, exposure, and the apparent hopelessness of further resistance led to increasing desertion, especially among recent conscripts. In March 1865 the Confederates were driven back at the Battle of Fort Stedman, leaving Lee with 50,000 troops as opposed to Grant's 120,000. Soon after, Grant crushed a main Southern force under General George E. Pickett and General Fitzhugh Lee at the Battle of Five Forks (April 1); the next day the defenders were driven back within the Petersburg inner defenses. Lee immediately informed President Jefferson Davis that the two cities could no longer be held, and the evacuation was carried out that night. After Lee's plan to join with General Joseph E. Johnston was thwarted, he surrendered to General Grant on April 9 at Appomattox Court House.

impassable desert called no-man's-land, where artillery fire soon eliminated habitation and vegetation alike. The fighting involved masses of men, masses of artillery, and masses of casualties. Toxic gases—asphyxiating, lachrymatory, and vesicant—were introduced in a vain effort to break the dominance of the defense, which was so overpowering that for more than two years the opposing lines varied less than 10 miles in either direction.

During the winter of 1916–17, the Germans prepared a reserve trench system, the Hindenburg Line, containing deep dugouts where the men could take cover against artillery fire and machine guns emplaced in concrete shelters called pillboxes. Approximately two miles behind the forward line was a second position, almost as strong. The Hindenburg Line resisted all Allied assaults in 1917, including a vast British mining operation under the Messines Ridge in Belgium that literally blew up the ridge, inflicting 17,000 casualties at one blow; the advance failed to carry beyond the ridge.

PERMANENT FORTIFICATION DURING WORLD WAR I

Most defensive thinking on the eve of World War I was reserved for the permanent fort, which was designed to canalize enemy advance and to afford time for national mobilization. The leading fortification engineer of the time was a Belgian, Henri Brialmont. He placed his forts, built of concrete, at an average distance of four miles from a city, as with 12 forts at Liège, and at intervals of approximately 4 km (2.5 miles). At Antwerp his defense system was even more dense. He protected the big guns of his forts with turrets of steel and developed disappearing cupolas. Some forts were pentagonal, others triangular, with much of the construction underground.

In building defenses along the frontier facing Germany, French engineers emulated Brialmont, with particularly strong clusters of fortresses at Verdun and Belfort. So monstrous were the forts of the time that they were known as "land battleships." But by marching through Belgium with a strong right wing (the Schlieffen plan), the Germans circumvented the powerful French fortresses. Passing between the forts at Liège, which Brialmont had intended to be connected with trenches, they took the city in only three days, then systematically reduced the forts. Namur, also heavily fortified, resisted the powerful Big Bertha guns for only four days. The concrete of the Belgian fortifications crumbled under the pounding, but the French forts at Verdun, of more recent and sturdier construction, later absorbed tremendous punishment and served as focal points for some of the war's bloodiest fighting.

THE MAGINOT LINE AND THE WEST WALL IN WORLD WAR II

In the interval between world wars, several European countries built elaborate permanent fortifications. The largest was the French Maginot Line, a system of mammoth, self-contained forts stretching from Switzerland to the vicinity of the Belgian frontier near Montmédy. The reinforced concrete of the forts was thicker than any theretofore used, the disappearing guns bigger and more heavily armoured. Ditches, embedded steel beams, and minefields guarded against tank attack. A large part of the works were completely underground. Outposts were connected to the main forts by concrete tunnels. But, because French and British military leaders were convinced that if war came again with Germany the Allies would fight in Belgium, the French failed to extend the line to the sea, relying instead on an outmoded system of unconnected fortresses left over from before World War I. It was this weakness that the Germans subsequently exploited in executing a modified version of the Schlieffen plan, cutting in behind the permanent defenses and defeating France without having to come to grips with the Maginot Line.

OTHER FORT SERIES

Elsewhere in World War II many fortifications similar to the Maginot Line and the West Wall were built. The Italians constructed a series of new fortifications and modernized existing World War I defenses along the country's mountainous northern and northeastern frontiers; the Finns maintained a World War I defense facing the Soviet Union, the Mannerheim Line (named after a Finnish marshal and statesman); the Soviets built the Stalin Line facing Poland; the Czechoslovaks constructed what became known as the Little Maginot Line to oppose Germany; the Greeks built the Metaxas Line facing Bulgaria; and the Belgians erected a series of elaborate forts along the Albert Canal. German capture of the most elaborate and allegedly impregnable of the Belgian forts, Eben Emael, in a matter of hours in the first two days of the campaign against France and the Low Countries in 1940 startled the world. Arriving silently on the night of May 10 in gliders, troops landed atop the fort and began systematically to destroy turrets and casemates. Soon after daylight they were joined by 300 men arriving by parachute. Around noon of May 11 the 1,000-man garrison surrendered.

Despite at least comparable surprise and the same so-called blitzkrieg methods, the Germans required more time to penetrate the more dispersed forts of the Stalin Line in the Soviet Union. The delay gained two months of invaluable time for the Soviet troops, without which they might well have been unable to stop the Germans at the gates of Moscow.

The Germans confronted that portion of the Maginot Line facing the Saar River with fortifications of their own, the West Wall. Later extended northward to the Dutch frontier and southward along the Rhine to Switzerland, the West Wall was not a thin line of big forts but a deep band, up to 8 km (5 miles) thick, of more than 3,000 small, mutually supporting pillboxes, observation posts, and troop shelters. For passive antitank defense the line depended upon natural obstacles, such as rivers and lakes, and upon "dragon's teeth," five rows of pyramid-shaped reinforced concrete projections.

The Germans did not rely on the West Wall to halt an attack but merely to delay it until counterattacks by mobile reserves could eliminate any penetration. The value of their concept remains undetermined; the line was not attacked until late 1944, after the German armies had incurred severe defeats and lacked adequate reserves. The West Wall nevertheless forced Allied troops into costly attacks to eliminate it.

GERMAN CHANNEL DEFENSES IN WORLD WAR II

The Germans employed Fritz Todt, the engineer who had designed the West

Wall, and thousands of impressed labourers to construct permanent fortifications along the Belgian and French coasts facing the English Channel; this was the Atlantic Wall. The line consisted primarily of pillboxes and gun emplacements embedded in cliffsides or placed on the waterfronts of seaside resorts and ports. Included were massive blockhouses with disappearing guns, newsreels of which the Germans sent out through neutral sources in an effort to awe their adversaries, but the numbers of big blockhouses actually were few. Behind the line, in likely landing spots for gliders and parachutists, the Germans emplaced slanted poles, which the troops called *Rommelsspargel* (Rommel's asparagus), after their commander Field Marshal Erwin Rommel. Embedded in the sand of the beaches below the high-tide mark were numerous obstacles, varying in shape and depth, some topped with mines. Barbed wire and antitank and antipersonnel mines interlaced the whole. On the French southwestern and southern coasts similar, though less formidable, defenses were erected.

When the Allies landed in force on the Cotentin Peninsula of Normandy on D-Day—June 6, 1944—they found the defenses far less formidable than they had anticipated. This was attributable to a number of reasons. The Germans had constructed the strongest defenses in the Pas-de-Calais region facing the narrowest part of the English Channel and had stationed their most battleworthy troops there, and the demands of other fighting fronts had siphoned many of the best German troops from France. The Germans also lacked air and naval support. Allied airpower was so strong that movement of German reserves was seriously impeded. Landings of Allied airborne troops behind the beaches spread confusion in German ranks. Also, the Germans were deluded into believing the invasion was a diversion, that a second and larger invasion was to follow in the Pas-de-Calais.

Only at one of the two American beaches, given the code name Omaha, was the success of the landing ever in doubt, partly because of rough seas, partly because of the chance presence of an elite German division, and partly because of the presence of high bluffs. Paradoxically, the Allies had less difficulty with the highly publicized beach defenses than they had later with field fortifications based on the Norman hedgerows, wide earthen embankments about 1.5 metres (5 feet) high that local farmers through the centuries had erected around thousands of irregularly shaped little fields to fence their cattle and protect their crops from strong ocean winds.

NUCLEAR FORTIFICATION

At the close of World War II most military theorists considered that permanent fortifications of the type previously employed were economically impracticable in view of their vulnerability to the incredible power of nuclear explosives and the methods, such as vertical envelopment from the air, that might be employed to reduce them. Important exceptions to this generalization were the reinforced concrete and deep tunnels used to protect strategic-missile launch facilities. During the Cold War the United States and the Soviet Union, as well as (to a lesser degree) France, Great Britain, Israel, and China, invested heavily in such defensive works.

Probably the most important and most characteristic of these works was the missile silo, a tubular structure of heavily reinforced concrete sunk into the ground to serve as a protective installation and launch facility for a single intercontinental ballistic missile (ICBM). These silos were "hardened" to resist a calculated amount of blast and shock from a nuclear detonation. Launch crews were protected in similarly constructed underground bunkers nearby. Elaborate calculations on the number of ICBM warheads needed to destroy a hardened silo with a given degree of certainty became an integral part of the strategic calculus in the 1960s. In this way, permanent fortifications resumed their previous place of importance in strategic calculations.

Of particular concern to strategists of the United States and the Soviet Union was the vulnerability of land-based ICBMs to preemptive nuclear attack. Elaborate defensive works were proposed to protect them. One basing scheme involved a network of fortified missile shelters connected by roads or railroad tracks. Huge, closed missile transporters would shuttle the missiles from one shelter to another in such a manner that the enemy would not know which shelters were occupied and which were empty. An even more extreme plan for protecting the U.S. land-based ICBM force was designed around fratricide, the theory that multiple nuclear explosions cannot occur at the same time in close proximity to one another because the first detonated warhead triggers low-yield partial explosions in the others. The proposal, called dense pack, would exploit this phenomenon by packing a large number of super-hardened ICBM silos closely together in a single location.

Other permanent fortifications of the nuclear age were designed as headquarters sites or command and control installations. For example, a joint U.S.-Canadian project, the North American Air Defense Command (Norad), included a series of radar posts across northern Canada and Alaska to provide early warning of the approach of hostile bombers or missiles. The system and the aircraft and missiles supporting it were controlled from a vast underground complex embedded in the rock of Cheyenne Mountain near Colorado Springs, Colo.

BODY ARMOUR

As mentioned, gunpowder weapons had made the heavy and expensive armoured suits of the medieval period obsolete,

U.S. marines battling for control of a ridge near Naha, Okinawa, May 1945.
U.S. Department of Defense

so that from the Renaissance onward armies increasingly opted not to outfit their soldiers with body armour in order to improve their stamina and ability to engage in long marches. However, the introduction of trench warfare during World War I and the devastating effects of artillery barrages caused armies once again to outfit their soldiers with metal combat helmets to protect against fragmentation wounds to the head. The German army even outfitted some soldiers in exposed positions—machine gunners, snipers, and sentries—with steel breastplates. Steel helmets were standard-issue for foot soldiers during World War II as well. In addition, bomber crews in that conflict wore heavy "flak jackets" designed to protect against fragmentation from air-defense guns.

The trend toward some modernized version of body armour has only accelerated with the arrival of deadlier weapons since World War II. Modern warfare subjects soldiers to a variety of lethal projectiles. Bullets fired from rifles, pistols, and machine guns can penetrate flesh and often create terrible wounds by "tumbling" when they hit a hard substance such as bone. Shell fragments—jagged pieces of metal formed by the explosion of a grenade or artillery projectile—can inflict substantial damage to the human body. Mines, booby traps, and improvised explosive devices target soldiers at close range and kill or wound through the force of explosion or the effects of fragmentation. Some of these devices are designed to penetrate vehicle armour with streams of molten metal; soldiers in the path of these metallic streams often suffer death, serious injury, or amputation of limbs.

As a result of these developments, soldiers in modern war suffer far more wounds from projectiles and fragmentation than from slicing or stabbing, as was the case before the advent of gunpowder and high explosives. All unprotected portions of the body are vulnerable to modern weaponry, but protection of the head and torso is especially necessary to prevent serious injury or death. To protect these critical areas of the body, modern armed forces have developed combat helmets and body armour for use by members of the armed forces on the battlefield, in combat aircraft, and in naval vessels.

NEW MATERIALS

The design of usable personal armour became possible with the arrival of synthetic materials that went beyond the heavy steel and thick leather used early in the 20th century. In the latter stages of the Korean War, the U.S. Army introduced the M-1952 armoured vest. The M-1952 weighed 8 pounds (3.6 kg), and its 12 layers of flexible, laminated nylon provided a measure of ballistic protection against shell fragments. U.S. soldiers and marines continued to wear the vest into the Vietnam War as well, until the Army replaced it with the Fragmentation Protective Body Armor, M-1969, which incorporated some minor improvements over the M-1952 but retained essentially the same protective characteristics as the older vest.

In the decades since the Vietnam War, the development of new materials such as Kevlar and advanced ceramics has given engineers the ability to create lightweight body armour that is effective against both fragmentation and bullets. Advanced fibres absorb the impact of bullets or fragments and disperse their energy across a large area as the projectiles move through successive layers of material. The bullets or fragments deform, or "mushroom," rather than penetrate the material. Likewise, a bullet's energy dissipates as it passes through a ceramic plate. A soft vest of tightly woven or laminated fibres thus provides basic protection against handgun rounds, small-calibre rifle rounds, and grenade fragments, and the addition of ceramic plates into pockets in the soft vest enables protection against high-velocity rifle rounds. Ballistic vests are generally rated using a system that classifies the degree of protection offered, from Type I (proof against .22-inch rifle bullets) to Type IV (proof against .30-inch armour-piercing rifle bullets).

Soldiers in Western-style armies now routinely enter into combat outfitted with a helmet (now often made of lightweight Kevlar rather than the older steel) to protect the head and with body armour (incorporating both Kevlar and ceramic) to protect the torso. Law-enforcement personnel routinely wear lightweight vests protective against handguns, and bomb-disposal experts wear even heavier suits designed to give them extensive full-body protection against explosions at close range.

MODERN BODY ARMOUR SYSTEMS

In the 1980s the U.S. Army developed the Personnel Armor System for Ground Troops (PASGT), which was composed of a newly designed Kevlar helmet and a Kevlar vest. Although the vest weighed 4 kg (9 pounds), slightly more than the M-1969 vest it replaced, it provided superior protection against shell fragments. In 2003, coinciding with the beginning of the Iraq War, the Army replaced the PASGT with the Interceptor Body Armor, or IBA, system. The IBA consists of an "outer tactical vest" made from layered Kevlar, which provides protection against shell fragments and most handgun bullets as large as 9 mm, and two ceramic "small arms protective inserts,"

or SAPI plates, which can be inserted into the vest to provide additional protection. Altogether the full system weighs some 7.25 kg (16 pounds), but it provides protection against 7.62-mm (.30-inch) full-metal-jacket rifle bullets—a level of protection that earlier versions of body armour could not provide.

The basic IBA system protects the body's most vital organs from injury, while the Kevlar helmet protects the head. Add-on components include a groin protector, a throat protector, and upper-arm protection. To counter a growing threat from improvised explosive devices and armour-piercing bullets, the U.S. military produced enhanced SAPI plates, enhanced side ballistic inserts, and deltoid and axillary protectors for the outer tactical vest, thus providing a greater area of body coverage and protecting against more-potent projectiles.

In the British armed forces body armour has gone through a similar evolution. Steel helmets, which had been standard-issue since World War I, were replaced in the 1980s by the first of a series of helmets fabricated of nylon. In the late 1980s a lightweight Combat Body Armour (CBA) was introduced, consisting of a vest with soft ballistic filler capable of protecting against fragments and 9-mm pistol rounds. The Enhanced Body Armour (EBA) version could be reinforced with ceramic plates for greater protection against higher-velocity projectiles. In response to combat conditions in the Afghanistan War, where

A U.S. Navy hospital corpsman wearing a full set of Interceptor Body Armor during a response to a simulated attack by an improvised explosive device, Fort Jackson, S.C., U.S. Courtesy of the U. S. Navy. Photo by Mass Communication Specialist 1st Class R. Jason Brunson

troops found themselves fighting more often on foot than in armoured vehicles, the Osprey Assault body armour system was introduced. This advanced system used slimmer ceramic plates and was to be worn with a new helmet design that allowed greater range of movement in prone firing positions.

The use of IBA- and Osprey-type systems has significantly reduced torso wounds and saved many lives in combat, but protection comes at the cost of decreased mobility and increased weight (and therefore decreased comfort and stamina) for individual soldiers. A complete set of enhanced IBA with all inserts and add-on components weighs more than 15 kg (33 pounds), and the Osprey Assault kit weighs only slightly less at almost 12.5 kg (28 pounds)—perhaps acceptable for the driver of a cargo truck but a considerable burden for an infantryman patroling on foot in the extreme heat of a Middle Eastern or South Asian summer. Some infantrymen complain that too much body armour is detrimental to fighting lightly armed and mobile guerrillas. Nevertheless, the benefits in most cases outweigh the disadvantages, so that body armour will likely remain part of the soldier's kit for the foreseeable future.

CHAPTER 5

MODERN SMALL ARMS: SHOULDER WEAPONS AND PISTOLS

Since the introduction of the flintlock musket in the 17th century, military small arms have gone through a series of significant changes. By employing different projectiles and successively improved chemical propellants, the dual goal of most arms designers has been the creation of man-portable weapons of greater firepower and reduced weight. But the attainment of this goal has continually been hampered by an inescapable physical relationship between the recoil forces generated by gunpowder weapons and the mass and velocity of their projectiles. In order to reduce the weight of a weapon, its recoil energy has to be reduced, but reducing recoil also affects the killing power of the bullet. Given the constraints of this relationship, military small arms may well have reached a level where, within reasonable economic limits, significantly higher performance cannot be obtained merely by improving existing gunpowder-based technology.

SHOULDER WEAPONS

The primary weapon of the infantryman since the invention of gunpowder has been some sort of small arm raised to the shoulder, aimed, and fired with some expectation of accuracy. Beginning with the flintlock musket, infantry shoulder weapons—progressing through muzzle-loaded smoothbores through breechloading rifles to modern assault rifles—have grown steadily in reliability and accuracy even as they have been reduced in size.

SMOOTHBORE MUZZLE-LOADERS

Practical shoulder-fired small arms started with the perfection of the flintlock ignition system in the mid-17th century. Earlier gunpowder small arms, based on the matchlock or wheel lock mechanisms, were generally too heavy, too unreliable, or too expensive to allow for general issue to infantry forces. Indeed, the first matchlock *mosquetes* ("muskets") fielded by Spanish infantry weighed as much as 10 kg (25 pounds) and usually required a forked staff as a rest to enable a man of normal strength to fire them accurately from the shoulder. Nevertheless, they were capable of sending bullets through the best armour that could be worn by a mobile soldier. Almost overnight, firepower from muskets became the dominant force in war, and fully armoured soldiers almost disappeared from European battlefields toward the end of the 16th century. With armour-piercing power no longer necessary, muskets could be made smaller, and shoulder weapons without rests became the norm.

The introduction of new ignition systems did not immediately render older forms obsolete, however; all systems, in many variations, existed side by side. Wheel locks and matchlocks, for example, persisted into the 18th century, long after flintlocks had established their primacy in Europe and America.

STANDARDIZED PATTERNS AND PARTS

Flintlock small arms emerged at the start of industrialization, with weapons production becoming one of the first industrial sectors to exploit the transition from craft production to the large-scale production of the Industrial Revolution. On the military side, these weapons entered service at a time when the scale of ground forces employed in battle was increasing. The ability to manufacture large numbers of muskets enabled military leaders to equip these mass armies.

By the 1600s European military authorities had begun moving toward greater uniformity in order to eliminate mixed inventories of nonstandard weapons. England took the first steps toward creating a national system of small-arms manufacture. For years, completed muskets had been purchased from a variety of English, Irish, and Dutch gunmakers, who subcontracted for components and arranged for final assembly. Beginning in the early 1700s, ordnance officials, from their headquarters at the Tower of London, divided the manufacture of firearms into locks, stocks, barrels, ramrods, and furniture—all of which they sought to purchase directly from subcontractors. Since different components for the same weapon were made in different locations, Tower officials oversaw the establishment of "Sealed Patterns" (sample firearms) to serve as exact models for gunmakers.

An Ordnance Office decree of 1722 led to a standard army musket, called the "Long Land," which had a 117-cm (46-inch) barrel and a calibre, or bore diameter, of 19 mm (.75 inch). The Long Land became popularly known in America as the first model Brown

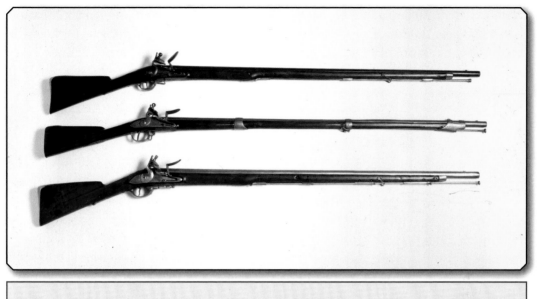

Rifles used during the American Revolution included the "Long Land" service musket (bottom), commonly known in America as the Brown Bess. MPI/Archive Photos/Getty Images

Bess musket. Fighting experience in the wilderness of North America during the Seven Years' War, or French and Indian War (1756–63), suggested the utility of lighter and shorter muskets, and in 1768 the Short Land musket, with a 106-cm (42-inch) barrel, became standard. Known as the second model Brown Bess, the Short Land became one of the basic weapons used in the American Revolution (1775–83). It was succeeded in 1797 by the "India Pattern," with a 99-cm (39-inch) barrel. During the wars with Napoleon from 1804 to 1815, more than 1.6 million of these muskets were assembled in Birmingham, and nearly 2.7 million muskets of all types were "fitted up" in London and at the Lewisham Royal Armoury Mills. In 1816 assembly work was divided between London and a

new Royal Small Arms Factory at Enfield Lock, Middlesex.

In France, standard-pattern muskets did not exist prior to 1717, when the government specified a weapon with a 120-cm (47-inch) barrel and a calibre of 17.53 mm (.69 inch). (This calibre remained standard until the 19th century.) After the Seven Years' War, the French army introduced the Modèle 1763, with a stronger lock and shorter (45-inch, or 114-cm) barrel—a length that remained standard to century's end. The Modèle 1777 musket represented a major step forward because of improved production techniques, with the French creating a rigorous system of patterns and gauges that yielded muskets with nearly interchangeable parts. This process was intended to produce less expensive muskets that were easier to make and repair, but worker resistance delayed large-scale manufacture of small arms using interchangeable parts until the early 1800s. Had the program succeeded earlier, France would have been better equipped to fight the Napoleonic Wars. As it was, French firms in such provincial cities as Charleville, Maubeuge, Saint-Étienne, and Tulle fabricated fewer than two million small arms.

The U.S. government created national armouries at Springfield, Mass., and at Harpers Ferry, Va., in 1794; work at Springfield commenced in 1795, and arms production began at Harpers Ferry in 1801. Both built an Americanized version of the French Modèle 1777 musket (known as the Model 1795 in the United States). These armouries and their private competitors later became important centres of technological innovation. With the adoption of the 17.53 mm (.69-inch) Model 1842, the U.S. military introduced the large-scale assembly of weapons from uniform, interchangeable parts. By the mid-1850s arms makers around the world were beginning to copy this "American System" of manufacture, which contributed to the creation of the modern military small arm—especially after the introduction of percussion ignition and rifled barrels.

PERCUSSION IGNITION

The Model 1842 was based on the Model 1840 flintlock, but it featured a switch to percussion ignition. This newer system was based on the explosive property of potassium chlorate and fulminate of mercury, both of which detonate when struck a small, sharp blow by a striker. Several Germans experimented with detonating fulminates in the late 17th century, and the French did likewise in the 18th century, but it was Alexander John Forsyth, a Scottish clergyman, who successfully wedded priming powders to the ignition of firearms in 1805, receiving a patent in April 1807. Forsyth invented the "scent bottle" type of lock mechanism, so called because rotating on a tapered steel plug at about the location of a flintlock touchhole was a powder-filled container that looked like a perfume bottle. Turning the bottle upside down released some detonator powder into a cavity at the top of the plug, and turning the bottle back left the striker mechanism, consisting of a hammer rather than the cock and jaws of the flintlock, free to operate. When the trigger was pulled, the hammer fell, detonating the compound.

Subsequent inventors simplified the percussion lock mechanism by using loose or pellet detonating powder. By 1830, percussion caps (attributed to the Philadelphian Joshua Shaw in 1815) were becoming the accepted system for igniting firearm powder charges. A percussion cap was a truncated cone of metal (preferably copper) that contained a small amount of fulminate of mercury inside its crown, protected by foil and shellac. This cap was fitted onto a steel nipple mounted at the weapon's breech, and a small channel in the nipple communicated the flash from the cap to the powder chamber. In the final form of this mechanism, a hollow-nosed percussion hammer came down over the percussion cap, thus eliminating the danger of flying copper when the powder detonated. Percussion cap ignition was easily adapted to existing flintlock muskets and pistols.

RIFLED MUZZLE-LOADERS

As killing machines, smoothbore infantry muskets were relatively inefficient. Their heavy, round lead balls delivered bone-crushing and tissue-destroying blows when they hit a human body, but beyond 68 metres (75 yards) even trained infantrymen found it difficult to hit an individual adversary. Volley fire against massed troops delivered effective projectiles out to 182 metres (200 yards), but at 274 metres (300 yards) balls from muzzle-loaders lost most of their lethality. Also, while well-trained soldiers could load and shoot their muskets five times per minute, volley fire led to a collective rate of only two to three shots per minute.

These ballistic shortcomings were a product of the requirement that the projectile, in order to be quickly rammed from muzzle to breech, had to fit loosely in the barrel. When discharged, it wobbled down the barrel, contributing to erratic flight after it left the muzzle. The solution to this problem lay in the rifled barrel.

EARLY RIFLING

Rifled barrels, in which spiral grooves were cut into the bore, had long been known to improve accuracy by imparting a gyroscopic spin to the projectile, but reloading rifled weapons was slowed because the lead ball had to be driven into the barrel's rifling. Greased cloth or leather patches eased the problem somewhat, but the rate of fire of rifles was still much lower than that of smoothbore muskets. One possible solution was the creation of mechanisms that allowed the bullet to be loaded at the breech instead of the muzzle. Many such ideas were tested during the 18th century, but, given the craftsman-based manufacture of the day, none was suited to large-scale production. Special army units in Europe and America used rifled muzzle-loaders, such as the flintlock British Baker rifle, to harass the enemy at long ranges, while most infantrymen continued to carry muzzle-loading smoothbores.

For this reason, inventors concentrated on adapting rifled barrels to muzzle-loaders. In 1826 Henri-Gustave Delvigne of France, seeking a means of expanding the projectile without making it difficult to ram home, created a narrow powder chamber at the breech end of the barrel against which a loosely fitting lead ball came to rest. Ramrod blows expanded the soft lead at the mouth of the chamber so that, when fired, the bullet fit the rifling tightly. In 1844 another French officer, Louis-Étienne de Thouvenin, introduced yet a better method for expanding bullets. His *carabine à tige* embodied a post or pillar (*tige*) at the breech against which the bullet was expanded.

MINIÉ RIFLES

These rifles worked better than earlier types, but their deformed balls flew with reduced accuracy. Captain Claude-Étienne Minié, inspired by Delvigne's later work with cylindrical bullets, designed longer, smaller-diameter projectiles, which, having the same weight as larger round balls, possessed greater cross-sectional density and therefore retained their velocity better. Moreover, while the flat base of Minié's projectile was deformed against the pillar as in Thouvenin's weapon, the rest of the bullet maintained its shape and accuracy. The French army combined these ideas in the Carabine Modèle 1846 à tige and the Fusil d'Infanterie Modèle 1848 à tige.

In order to combat the tendency of muzzle-loading rifles to become difficult to load as gunpowder residue collected in the barrels, Minié suggested a major simplification—eliminating the pillar and employing in its place a hollow-based bullet with an iron expander plug that caused the projectile to engage the rifling when the weapon was fired. This new projectile could be loaded into dirty rifles with ease, and, because it was not deformed while loading, it had greater accuracy.

Officials in several countries, notably Britain and the United States, saw the significance of Minié's invention. In 1851 the Royal Small Arms Factory, Enfield, embarked upon production of the 17.83 mm (.702 inch) Pattern 1851 Minié rifle. In the Crimean War (1854–56), Russian

A cover of Harper's Weekly magazine during the American Civil War, depicting African American recruits to the Union Army being trained in the use of the Minie rifle. Library of Congress Prints and Photographs Division

troops armed with smoothbore muskets were no match for Britons shooting P/51 rifles. Massed formations were easy prey, as were cavalry and artillery units. A correspondent for the *Times* of London wrote: "The Minié is king of weapons . . . the volleys of the Minié cleft [Russian soldiers] like the hand of the Destroying Angel."

Swiss experiments demonstrated that an expander plug was not necessary when a bullet's side walls were thin enough, and the British designed a smaller-calibre rifle using this type of Minié bullet. The result was a 14.6 mm

(.577 inch) weapon firing "cylindro-conoidal" projectiles—essentially a lead cylinder with a conical nose. "Enfield" as a weapon name was first generally applied to these Pattern 1853 rifles. Subsequent tests indicated that rifles with 84-cm (33-inch) barrels could provide accuracy equal to the 99-cm (39-inch) P/53 barrels. When the resulting P/53 Short Rifles were issued, there began a century-long trend toward shorter weapons.

In the United States, experiments undertaken in the late 1840s led to the adoption of a 14.73-mm (.58-inch) Minié-type bullet and a family of arms designed to use it. The Model 1855 rifled musket, with a 102-cm (40-inch) barrel, produced a muzzle velocity of 290 metres (950 feet) per second. All Model 1855 weapons used mechanically operated tape priming, intended to eliminate the manual placement of percussion caps on the nipple, but this system proved too fragile and was eliminated with the introduction of a simplified Model 1861 rifled musket. During the American Civil War (1861–65), the Union government purchased both Model 1861 and Model 1863 rifled muskets as its basic infantry weapon. In the Confederacy, domestic production was supplemented by purchases of Enfield P/53 rifles and other European weapons.

The Civil War clearly demonstrated the deadly effect of rifled muskets, although many battlefield commanders only slowly appreciated the changing nature of warfare. Individual soldiers could hit their opposing numbers with accurate fire out to 250 yards (225 metres),

so that frontal assaults, in which soldiers advanced in neat ranks across open fields, had to be abandoned. By 1862 both sides were building field entrenchments and barricades to provide protection from rifle and artillery fire.

BREECHLOADERS

The American Civil War also previewed the importance of breech-loading rifles. For more than a century, soldiers carrying muzzle-loaders had been issued paper cartridges containing the musket ball and an appropriate powder charge. To use one of these cartridges, they simply bit off the end of the paper tube, poured a little powder into the pan (if the gun was a flintlock), dumped the rest down the barrel, and then rammed the ball and paper down on top. Some early breechloaders used slightly improved cartridges of nitrate-soaked paper or linen that contained the powder and ball and were inserted into the opened breech as a unit. The powder was set off when sparks from the flashpan ignited either the flammable case itself or exposed powder at the end of the cartridge. Other breechloaders employed metal cartridges that were pierced with holes or made with ends of flammable paper, so that the powder could be ignited by a percussion cap. But all of these systems, which relied upon externally mounted flintlock or percussion ignition mechanisms, were prone to misfiring, and they did little to prevent the leakage of gas and flame for which breechloaders were notorious.

THE BOLT ACTION

Breech-loading rifles became practical only with the design of cartridges that housed the primer as well as the propellant in a single case, and that provided an effective seal when the weapon was fired. The first such cartridge to be successfully employed in war was of the rimfire type, in which a ring of detonating fulminate was deposited in a hollow rim around the base of a thin copper case. An external hammer crushed the rim in one spot, firing the round. Unfortunately, some fulminate compounds detonated unpredictably, leading to both misfires and premature explosions. Also, a cartridge case that was soft enough to be crushed by a striker could not stand up to the heavy propellant charge necessary for a full-power infantry rifle. For this reason, rimfire cartridges were used most effectively in pistols or—during the American Civil War—in smaller repeating carbines such as the 14.22-mm (.56-inch) Spencer and the 11.18-mm (.44-inch) Henry.

In Europe, a milestone in the development of breech-loading infantry weapons was achieved by Johann Nikolaus Dreyse, a Prussian. His *Zündnadelgewehr* ("needle-fired gun"), introduced in 1838, used a paper cartridge with a priming pellet located at the base of a solid egg-shaped bullet. A long, needle-shaped firing pin, shot forward by a spring, pierced the cartridge and powder charge to detonate the primer. This needle was housed in a steel cylinder called the bolt, which slid forward in the frame of the receiver until it was locked firmly against the base of the cartridge in the chamber. Once the weapon was fired, the soldier released a latch with his thumb, grasped a knob at the end of a handle projecting from the bolt, turned it until locking lugs on the bolt were disengaged from slots in the receiver, and slid the bolt back to open the chamber for reloading. This bolt action, simple in concept and yet requiring precise workmanship, constituted a revolution in small-arms design.

The first Dreyse rifles were adopted by the Prussian army in 1843 and were used in campaigns in 1849 and 1864. In 1866, notably at the Battle of Königgrätz during the Seven Weeks' War, Prussian soldiers lying prone were able to fire six shots from their 15.43-mm (.607-inch) Zündnadelgewehr Modell 1862 for every one discharged from their Austrian opponents' muzzle-loading rifles.

Prussia's success encouraged other European states to adopt bolt-action breechloaders. The French employed Antoine-Alphonse Chassepot's 11-mm (.433-inch) Fusil d'Infanterie Modèle 1866 to devastating effect in such battles of the Franco-German War (1870–71) as Mars-la-Tour and Gravelotte. Close-order troop formations disappeared from the European scene as a result of these fights, and the cavalry charge was relegated to the past. The Chassepot rifle employed a shorter firing pin than the Dreyse, because its cartridge was fitted with a detonating cap at the very base. About 1.03 million of these weapons were in hand when the war began, and Prussia had some 1.15 million Dreyse needle rifles—a quantity that demonstrated the value of machine production of weapons with interchangeable parts.

Needle rifles offered a faster rate of fire, but their paper cartridges provided a poor seal at the breech, and their long firing pins warped or broke under heavy use. One solution was the metallic centre-fire cartridge with a percussion cap centred in the base of a hard brass or copper case. A shorter, sturdier firing pin was sufficient to detonate the primer, and a metallic case that was strong enough to withstand a powerful propellant charge also provided effective closure of the breech. Adopting centre-fire cartridges, France transformed its Chassepots into the 11-mm Modèle 1866/67 and 1874 rifles, which were named after their designer, Basile Gras. Germany went to rifles designed by Peter Paul Mauser, first the 11-mm (.433-inch) Modell 1871 Gewehr and then the Modell 1871/84 Infanterie-Repetier-Gewehr. The latter was a 10-shot repeater that ejected the spent case as the bolt was pulled back and fed a fresh cartridge into the chamber from a tubular magazine beneath the barrel as the bolt was pushed forward.

All other European countries soon adopted cartridge breech-loading rifles, usually by converting existing muzzle-loaders and then by purchasing purpose-built breechloaders. Many did not feature bolt action. For example, beginning in 1866, Britain converted its P/53 Enfields simply by hinging the top of the breech so that it could be opened sideways, the spent case extracted, and a fresh cartridge inserted. In 1871 the British went to new Martini-Henry breechloaders of 11.43-mm (.45-inch) calibre. In these rifles, pushing down a lever attached to the trigger guard lowered the entire breechblock, exposing the chamber, and raised the breechblock back to firing position when it was pulled back. Russia adopted two new 10-mm (.39-inch) breechloaders, the Model 1868 Berdan No. 1 and then the bolt-action Model 1870 Berdan No. 2, both of which were largely the work of American Civil War officer Hiram Berdan. The U.S.-made Remington Rolling Block Rifle, in which the breechblock was cocked back on a hinge like the hammer, was bought by a number of countries around the world. The United States itself adopted a series of single-shot rifles employing a hinged-breech "trap-door" mechanism, developed by Erskine S. Allin at the Springfield Armory, in which the top of the breech was flipped forward along the top of the barrel. The first Model 1866 was a converted 14.73-mm (.58-inch) musket, the second Model 1866 was a new rifle in 12.70-mm (.50-inch) calibre, and subsequent versions were built in 11.43-mm (.45-inch) calibre. These weapons, born of postwar starvation budgets, continued to use components introduced with the Model 1855 muzzle-loaders.

THE SMOKELESS-POWDER REVOLUTION

All early breechloaders used black powder as their source of propellant energy,

THE MANY USES OF GUNCOTTON

In 1833 Henry Braconnot, director of the Botanic Garden in Nancy, France, treated potato starch, sawdust, and cotton with nitric acid. Braconnot found that this material, which he called "xyloidine," was soluble in wood vinegar, and he attempted to make coatings, films, and shaped articles of it. In 1838 another French chemist, Théophile-Jules Pelouze, discovered that paper or cardboard could be made violently flammable by dipping it in concentrated nitric acid; Pelouze named his new material "pyroxyline." Christian Friedrich Schönbein, a Swiss chemist, was able to increase the degree of nitration, and therefore the flammability of the product, by dipping cotton in a mixture of nitric and sulfuric acids. In 1846 he announced the discovery of this revolutionary explosive substance—nitrocellulose, popularly known as guncotton—and acquired patents in Britain and the United States. Schönbein also described the dissolution of moderately nitrated cellulose in ether and ethyl alcohol to produce a syrupy fluid that dried to a transparent film; mixtures of this composition eventually found use as collodion, employed through the 19th century as a photographic carrier and antiseptic wound sealant.

Guncotton did not come into use as an ingredient of gunpowder until the 1860s. The early history of its use was punctuated by many disastrous explosions, caused partly by the failure to appreciate that nitrocellulose is an unstable material and is subject to catalytic decomposition caused by its own decomposition products. In 1868 English chemist Sir Frederick Augustus Abel showed that the methods then prevalent for washing nitrocellulose after nitration were inadequate and that the residual acid was causing instability. In the 1880s French engineer Paul Vieille added special stabilizers to nitrocellulose to neutralize the catalytically active decomposition products; the first stable and reliable propellant, smokeless powder, resulted from his work and became the main form of gunpowder.

Nitrated cellulose retains its threadlike shape even in solution, and, in the 19th century, methods were devised to spin nitrocellulose into fibres and then convert them back into cellulose. These efforts culminated in 1891 with the introduction of "Chardonnet silk," the first commercially produced artificial fibre and a type of rayon, by the French chemist Hilaire Bernigaud, comte de Chardonnet. In 1869 American inventor John W. Hyatt mixed solid pyroxylin and camphor to produce the first commercially successful plastic, known as celluloid, which he patented the next year. After World War I nitrocellulose was employed in paints for the booming auto industry. Although nitrocellulose coatings are no longer employed on a massive scale, owing to restrictions on the use of products that contain volatile organic compounds, nitrocellulose continues to be used as a film-forming polymer in certain specialty coatings.

but in the early 1880s more powerful and cleaner-burning nitrocellulose-based propellants were perfected. Whereas black powder produced a large quantity of solid material upon combustion, quickly fouling barrels and pouring out huge clouds of smoke, nitrocellulose produced mostly gas and was therefore labeled "smokeless powder." Also, it produced three times the energy of black powder and burned at a more controllable rate. Such characteristics made possible a shift to longer and smaller-diameter projectiles. Bore diameters were again reduced, this time to calibres of 7.5 to 8 mm, or about .30 inch. Muzzle velocities ranged from 600 to 850 metres (2,000 to 2,800 feet) per second, and accurate range extended to 900 metres (1,000 yards) and beyond. Because lead projectiles were too soft to be used at such increased power and velocity, they were sheathed in harder metal. In 1881 a Swiss officer, Eduard Alexander Rubin, was the first to perfect a full-length, copper-jacketed bullet.

MAGAZINE REPEATERS

France was the first country to issue a small-bore, high-velocity repeating rifle, the Modèle 1886 Lebel, which fired an 8-mm (.312-inch), smokeless-powder round. The tubular magazine of this rifle soon became obsolete, however. In 1885 Ferdinand Mannlicher of Austria had introduced a boxlike magazine fitted into the bottom of the rifle in front of the trigger guard. This magazine was easily loaded by a device called a clip, a light metal openwork box that held five cartridges and fed them up into the chamber through the action of a spring as each spent case was ejected. Other magazine rifles, such as the Mauser, used a different loading device, called a charger. This was simply a flat strip of metal with its edges curled to hook over the rims or grooves of a row of cartridges (also usually five). To load his rifle, a soldier drew back the bolt, slipped the charger into position above the opened receiver, and pushed the cartridges down into the magazine, where they were held in tension against a spring. The efficiency of the box magazine was quickly recognized, as was its special compatibility with the bolt action, and all European states made the conversion. For example, Germany adopted the 8-mm (.312-inch) Model 1888 Commission rifle, Belgium the 7.65-mm (.30-inch) Model 1889 Mauser, Turkey the Model 1890 Mauser, and Russia the 7.62-mm (.30-inch) Model 1891 Mosin-Nagant. In 1892 Britain abandoned movable-block action and went to the 7.70-mm (.303-inch), bolt-action Lee-Metford, and the United States began to purchase the .30-inch Model 1892 Krag-Jørgensen, a Danish design. In 1906 Japan adopted the 6.5-mm (.26-inch) Year 38 Arisaka rifle.

By World War I (1914–18) all major powers adopted smokeless-powder, bolt-action, magazine-fed repeating rifles, and some had shifted to a second generation. Austria, for example, issued the Modell 1895 Mannlicher, firing an 8-mm (.312-inch) round, and German troops carried the 7.92-mm (.31-inch) Modell 1898, designed by Mauser. For durability, safety, and efficiency, the 1898 Mauser was probably the epitome of bolt-action military rifles. It was sold and copied around the world. In the United States the Mauser was only slightly altered and issued as the .30-inch M1903 Springfield.

Also following Germany's lead in the design of ammunition, all armies replaced their blunt-nosed projectiles with aerodynamically superior pointed bullets (in German, *Spitzgeschossen*). Barrel lengths continued to decrease, partly in response to more efficient propellants and partly to make rifles easier to use in the field. The British 7.70-mm (.303-inch) Short, Magazine, Lee-Enfield rifle, known as the SMLE, had a 64-cm (25-inch) barrel, while the M1903 Springfield's barrel measured just over 60 cm (23.75 inches).

During the Great War, huge quantities of rifles were built. British factories made more than 3.9 million rifles, German sources produced about 5 million, and Russian factories built more than 9 million. Still, most armies suffered from shortages. Factories in the United States made 1.24 million rifles for the British and 280,000 for the Russians; for U.S. forces they produced 2.4 million between May 1917 and December 1918 alone.

AUTOMATIC WEAPONS

An automatic rifle is a weapon that utilizes either the energy or gas generated by a fired round to remove the spent cartridge case, load a new cartridge, and cock the weapon to fire again. Automatic rifles are sometimes called self-loaders or autoloaders and are actually semiautomatic, since they customarily fire only one shot at each pull of the trigger. Full automatic fire—that is, firing repeatedly as long as the trigger is held down until the magazine is exhausted—is achieved by the assault rifle and the submachine gun. In the assault rifle, fully automatic fire can be substituted for one-shot fire simply by flicking a switch on the weapon.

THE SELF-LOADING RIFLE

Magazine-fed rifles provided a radical increase in rate of fire. Indeed, by 1914 many British riflemen could fire 15 aimed shots per minute, and some very skillful individuals could exceed 30 shots per minute. Nevertheless, in order to transcend the limits imposed by manual operation, gun designers such as Mannlicher and the American Hiram Maxim came up with experimental self-loading, or semi-automatic, rifles, which used the energy generated by a fired round to load a fresh round into the chamber. However, only a handful of these weapons were adopted in very small numbers by the major armies, whose interest in automatic fire from the 1880s through World War I was directed primarily toward heavier infantry-support weapons.

After the war, all nations having an arms industry sought to produce a semiautomatic rifle, but only the United States was successful in developing and manufacturing a battle-worthy weapon. Adopted in 1936, the U.S. Rifle, Caliber .30 M1, designed by John C. Garand, was a technological tour de force. A small hole or gas port on the underside of its barrel near the muzzle directed part of the propellant gases into a small cylinder holding a piston that was connected to the bolt. As gas pressure forced back the piston and bolt, the empty cartridge case was ejected and the hammer was cocked. A spring then forced the bolt forward. As it moved forward, the bolt stripped the top cartridge from an eight-round, clip-loaded magazine within the receiver and seated it in the chamber, ready to fire. Gas pressure thus performed automatically the reloading task formerly done by hand.

As the only semiautomatic rifle to become a standard-issue infantry weapon, the M1 was extremely durable and reliable in combat. Between 1937 and 1945, the Springfield Armory and the Winchester Repeating Arms Company produced 4.04 million of these rifles. Still, the infantry units of most other belligerents during World War II (1939–45) were armed with bolt-action rifles of the World War I era as their standard weapons.

THE SUBMACHINE GUN

The ballistic performance of infantry rifles was tailored to the long-range requirements of a bygone era when foot soldiers demanded weapons that could reach out to halt the dreaded cavalry charge. Beginning early in World War I, however, battlefields became no-man's-lands pockmarked by shell craters and crisscrossed by miles of barbed-wire entanglements, and machine guns dominated the 1,000 or more yards between trench lines. While rifles were shot at those extreme ranges, they could not equal the destructive power of artillery and machine guns, and they were too cumbersome and powerful for offensive assaults on enemy trenches.

A generation later, in World War II, the greater mobility of troops accompanying armoured vehicles reinforced the need for lighter, more portable weapons of improved effectiveness at close quarters.

Such changing conditions led to experiments with automatic weapons firing rounds of lower velocity or lighter weight. One result, which saw its first use in World War I, was a new weapon called the machine carbine or submachine gun. Derived from the semiautomatic pistol and firing pistol-calibre ammunition with muzzle velocities of only about 300 metres (1,000 feet) per second, submachine guns were fitted with shoulder stocks (and sometimes forward hand grips). Such weapons offered easier handling than rifles while providing greater accuracy and more rapid fire than most handguns.

The first successful weapon of this type was the Maschinen Pistole 1918 Bergmann, designed by Hugo Schmeisser and employed by the Germans during the last few months of the war. The barrel of the MP18 was less than 20 cm (8 inches) long, and it was chambered for 9-mm (.35-inch) rounds introduced in 1908 for Parabellum, or Luger, pistols. It operated under a principle called blowback, in which the spent cartridge case, blown backward out of the chamber by the gases generated by the firing of the round, forced the bolt back against a spring and tripped the mechanism that ejected the case from the gun. The spring then forced the bolt forward as a fresh cartridge was fed into the chamber. If the trigger was kept depressed, the new round would be fired automatically, and the cycle would continue until the trigger was released or the ammunition was exhausted. In blowback actions, the bolt had to be quite heavy, or it had to be subjected to various devices that retarded its backward motion, in order to keep the mechanism from operating faster than was desired. In the MP18, a heavy bolt and spring limited the weapon's rate of fire to about 400 rounds per minute.

After the war, Vasily Degtyarev of the Soviet Union incorporated Schmeisser's principles into his own designs, culminating in the Pistolet Pulemyot Degtyarova of 1940. The PPD was fed by a drum-shaped magazine containing 71 7.62-mm (.30-inch) cartridges, and it fired at a rate of 900 rounds per minute—far too fast for accuracy. In the United States, John T. Thompson's submachine gun, chambered for the 11.43-mm (.45-inch) Colt pistol cartridge, was adopted by the army in 1928. Popularly called the "tommy gun," the M1928 was effective, but its blowback operation was modified by a complex retarding mechanism that was deleted from later versions, when its large drum magazine was also replaced by a box magazine.

Under the pressures of World War II, the major powers used millions of submachine guns. These included a second generation of simplified weapons that, being fabricated partly from sheet-metal stampings, could be produced in quantity almost anywhere and at little expense. The Germans led the way with the MP38 and MP40. Known to the Allies as "burp guns," these weapons operated at 450 to 550 rounds per minute, the optimal rate for controlled fire. Also, they were fed by a box magazine, which did not jam as often as a drum, and had a wire shoulder stock that could be folded against the receiver. Meanwhile, the Soviets issued en masse the PPSh of 1941 and the PPS of 1943. The latter closely resembled the new German guns, as did the United States' M3, called the "grease gun" for its resemblance to a mechanic's grease dispenser. The British Sten gun, extremely simple and inexpensive yet very effective, was issued to paratroops and commandos beginning in 1941 and was also smuggled to partisans in Europe.

After the war, almost all new submachine guns, such as the British Sterling and West German MP5, were chambered for 9-mm (.35-inch) cartridges. As a class of weapon, they received a new lease on life with the telescoping bolt, pioneered by Václav Holek in the Czechoslovak Model 23 of 1948. This involved a hollowed-out bolt that slid partially over the barrel when a round was chambered, resulting in a much shorter weapon. A prominent example of this type was the Israeli Uzi, designed by Uziel Gal, which was only 63.5 cm (25 inches) long with its shoulder stock extended. The Uzi was adopted around the world as a police and counterterrorist weapon. Indeed, aside from arming special forces, the submachine gun lost importance as a military weapon. With an effective range limited to about 180 metres (200 yards), it could not fill the broad gap between the low-power pistol cartridge and the full-power rifle cartridge. This gap, which constituted the ground upon which modern infantrymen found themselves fighting, had to be filled by another new weapon, which would fire a cartridge of intermediate power.

THE ASSAULT RIFLE

A hint at this new weapon had been given during World War I, when Vladimir Grigorevich Fyodorov, father of Russian automatic weapons, married the 6.5-mm (.26-inch) cartridge of the Japanese Arisaka rifle to an automatic rifle. In 1916 he unveiled his new weapon, the Avtomat Fyodorova. Owing to the turmoil of the Russian Revolution of 1917, only about 3,200 of Fyodorov's weapons were delivered. Nevertheless, they pointed the way to future infantry weapon design.

During World War II, Hugo Schmeisser designed a light rifle to fire the Germans' 7.92-mm (.31-inch) Kurz, or "Short," cartridge, which was of the same calibre as the Mauser rifle cartridge but was lighter and shorter and was therefore of a less potent, "intermediate" power. The weapon, known variously as the MP43, MP44, or Sturmgewehr ("Assault Rifle") 44, was loaded by a curved box magazine holding 30 rounds and was designed for most effective fire at about 270 metres (300 yards). Only 425,000 to 440,000 of these rifles were built—too few

and too late for the German war effort—but they were based on a concept that would dominate infantry weapons for the rest of the century.

Late in the war the Soviets also began a search for a rifle to shoot their 7.62-mm (.30-inch) intermediate cartridge, which produced a muzzle velocity of 710 metres (2,330 feet) per second. Historical evidence suggests that they were influenced by the Sturmgewehr, but to what extent remains uncertain. In 1947 they adopted a weapon designed by Mikhail Timofeyevich Kalashnikov, naming it the Avtomat Kalashnikova. Like the German weapon, the AK-47 was operated by diverting some of the propellant gases into a cylinder above the barrel; this drove a piston that forced the bolt back against its spring and cocked the hammer for the next round. At the turn of a selector switch, the action could be changed from semiautomatic to fully automatic, firing at a rate of 600 rounds per minute. The AK-47 was made of forged and milled steel, giving it a weight of 4.8 kg (10.6 pounds) with a loaded 30-round magazine. The receiver of the AKM version, introduced in 1959, was made of lighter sheet metal, reducing the weight to 3.8 kg (8.3 pounds), and the AK-74 version, following later trends in the West, switched to a 5.45-mm (.21-inch) cartridge with a higher muzzle velocity of 900 metres (about 3,000 feet) per second. The most recent version of the AK-74, the AK-74M, is currently the main infantry weapon of the Russian army.

Kalashnikov's assault rifles became the most significant infantry weapons of the post-World War II era. In many variants, they were adopted and made by countries all over the world. It has been estimated that some 100 million AKs have been produced since the series' introduction, more than any other firearm in history.

The development of Western small arms proceeded more slowly, mainly because the United States insisted upon maintaining a power level comparable to the M1. As a result, in 1953 the North Atlantic Treaty Organization (NATO) reluctantly agreed to standardize on a 7.62-mm (.30-inch) cartridge that was a half-inch shorter than the M1 cartridge but of the same calibre and power. To fire this new round, the United States produced an improved version of the M1 rifle, featuring a 20-round detachable magazine and being capable of selective fire. Called the U.S. Rifle 7.62mm M14, it replaced the M1, beginning in 1957. As a self-loading rifle the M14 performed well,

Toting an AK-47 for protection, a young Kurdish woman poses in the mountains of northern Iraq, 1979. Since its invention in 1947, the Kalashnikov rifle (AK-47) has been a popular weapon for rebel groups and established armies. Alex Bowie/Hulton Archive/Getty Images

but it was too heavy as a close-quarters weapon, and the extreme recoil generated by the NATO round caused it to be totally unmanageable as an automatic rifle.

Other NATO armies adopted more satisfactory 7.62-mm (.30-inch) rifles, although even these were employed as advanced self-loaders rather than automatics. Most commonly, they were either the gas-operated Fusil Automatique Léger (FAL), introduced by the Belgian Fabrique Nationale d'Armes de Guerre in 1957, or the blowback-operated Gewehr 3 (G3), produced in West Germany by the firm Heckler & Koch, beginning in 1959. Millions of these weapons were sold to many countries.

After the Korean War (1950–53), U.S. military researchers dissatisfied with rifle-power ammunition began to test a .22-inch (5.56-mm) cartridge that propelled a lighter projectile at a much higher muzzle velocity of 3,000 feet (about 900 metres) per second. To fire this "small-calibre, high-velocity" round, in 1958 they chose the AR-15 rifle, designed by Eugene M. Stoner for the ArmaLite Division of Fairchild Engine and Airplane Corporation. The AR-15 was gas-operated, but it eliminated the piston in favour of a tube that directed propellant gases directly into an expansion chamber between the bolt and bolt carrier. By reducing the number of working parts and chambering the rifle for a smaller cartridge, Stoner had come up with a lightweight weapon that, even on automatic fire, produced a manageable recoil and yet was capable of inflicting fatal wounds at 300 yards (270 metres) and beyond. In 1961 the air force purchased the AR-15, renaming it the M16. Six years later, with units in Vietnam finding the weapon very effective under the close conditions of jungle warfare, the army adopted it as the M16A1.

After U.S. troops in Europe were issued the M16, a series of trials ensued that ended with the decision, in 1980, to adopt a standard 5.56-mm (.22-inch) NATO cartridge. This fired a brass-jacketed projectile that, having a heavier lead core and steel nose, was lethal at longer ranges than the original AR-15 bullet. The M16A2, which has been the standard-issue infantry weapon of the U.S. military since the 1980s, was rifled to fire this round, and other NATO armies switched over. West Germany introduced the G41, a 5.56-mm (.22-inch) version of the G3, and Belgium replaced the FAL with the FNC. The British and French armies developed new assault rifles with compact "bullpup" designs, in which the bolt, receiver, and magazine were behind the handgrip and trigger and much of the shoulder stock was occupied by the operating mechanism. This permitted a much shorter weapon than orthodox designs, in which the magazine and receiver were ahead of the trigger. As a result, the French FA MAS and British L85A1 were only some 76 to 78 cm (30 to 31 inches) long—compared with the M16, which was 99 cm (39 inches) overall. Many of the newer models were built with lightweight plastic shoulder stocks and magazines, as well as receivers made of aluminum.

PISTOLS

Since the 16th century, soldiers have carried handguns to supplement their basic shoulder weapons. However, because the firepower of pistols must be kept low in order to reduce them to manageable weight, and because only skilled soldiers can shoot them accurately beyond 9 metres (10 yards), they have never been satisfactory military weapons. By World War II, pistols were issued principally to officers as a badge of rank and as a defensive weapon of last resort. Currently, they are most frequently carried by military police and other security personnel.

REVOLVERS

Until the mid-1840s most pistols were single-shot muzzle-loaders fired by wheel lock, flintlock, and percussion ignition systems. In 1835 Samuel Colt patented the first successful percussion revolver. In the frame of this weapon was a revolving cylinder drilled with several chambers (usually five or six), into which powder and ball (or combustible paper cartridges containing powder and ball) were loaded from the front. In the rear of each chamber a percussion cap was placed over a hollow nipple that directed the jet of flame to the powder when the cap was struck by the hammer. This type of revolver was eventually called "cap-and-ball." Where earlier revolvers required the shooter to line up a chamber with the barrel and cock the hammer in separate steps, Colt devised a single-action mechanical

linkage that rotated the cylinder as the hammer was cocked with the thumb.

Colt dominated the manufacture of revolvers until the expiration of his U.S. patent in 1857. At that time two other Americans, Horace Smith and Daniel B. Wesson, produced the first cartridge revolver, based on a design purchased from Rollin White. Using rim-fire copper cartridges and eliminating the percussion-cap nipple, this weapon could be quickly loaded from the rear.

When the Smith & Wesson patent expired in 1872, a host of new revolver designs appeared in the United States and Europe. The most important innovations were quick ejection of spent cartridges and double-action cocking. By linking the trigger to the hammer-cocking and cylinder-revolving mechanisms, double action permitted a pistol to be fired with a simple pull of the trigger. This mechanism was first introduced on a cap-and-ball revolver, the English Beaumont-Adams of 1855, but it was quickly adapted to cartridge revolvers. There were several mechanisms for removing spent cartridge cases. In the 1870s Smith & Wesson produced revolvers with hinged frames. When such a revolver was "broken open"—that is, when the barrel and cylinder were tipped on the hinge away from the hammer and handgrip—an ejector rod, located in the middle of the cylinder but having a star-shaped head that radiated into each chamber, pushed out all the cartridges simultaneously. In the 1890s some Colt revolvers were made with solid frames

Samuel Colt

When Samuel Colt, born in Hartford, Conn., on July 19, 1814, was a young seaman, he carved a wooden model of a revolver. Years later he perfected a working version that was patented in England and France in 1835 and in the United States the following year. Featuring a cartridge cylinder that was rotated by cocking the hammer, Colt's single-barreled pistols and rifles were slow to gain acceptance, and a company that formed to manufacture them in Paterson, N.J., failed in 1842. The following year he devised an electrically discharged naval mine, the first device using a remotely controlled explosive, and he also conducted a telegraph business that utilized the first underwater cable.

Word from military units that Colt's multi-shot weapons had been effective against Indians in Florida and Texas prompted a government order for 1,000 pistols during the Mexican War, and Colt resumed firearms manufacture in 1847. In 1855 he built the world's largest private armoury on the site of the present Colt Industries plant in Hartford. Assisted by Eli Whitney, Jr., he developed beyond any industrialist before him the manufacture of interchangeable parts and the production line, and he also applied progressive ideas concerning employee welfare. His invention made him a wealthy man. He died during the American Civil War, on Jan. 10, 1862, in Hartford. His firm produced the pistols most widely used during the Civil War, and its six-shot, single-action 11.43 mm (.45-inch) Peacemaker model, introduced in 1873, became the most famous sidearm of the West.

but with cylinders that swung out to the side, where pushing an ejector rod forced out the cartridges.

By the end of the 19th century the revolver had reached its definitive form and its highest possible effectiveness as a military weapon. Indeed, from the 1880s through World War II, British officers carried such revolvers as the 11.43-mm (.45-inch) Webley and the 9.65-mm (.38-inch) Enfield, both of which were the hinged-frame design. The U.S. military adopted various revolvers, usually Colts or Smith & Wessons of .38-inch or .45-inch calibre, until 1911, when it switched to autoloading pistols.

Self-Loaders

A high rate of fire was especially crucial to last-ditch, close-quarters defense, and, with handguns as well as shoulder arms, this meant automatic loading. Following Hiram Maxim's experiments with self-loading machine guns, automatic-pistol designs appeared in the last years of the 19th century.

In 1893 Ludwig Loewe & Company (later known as Deutsche Waffen- und Munitionsfabriken) introduced the first commercially viable self-loading pistol. Designed by an American, Hugo Borchardt, this 7.63-mm (.30-inch) weapon operated on the principle of recoil. When the gun was fired, the barrel and breechblock, locked together by a "toggle-link" mechanism, slid back together along the top of the frame. The toggle, essentially a two-piece arm hinged in the middle but lying flat behind the breechblock, also recoiled for a short distance before it was forced to buckle upward at its hinge. This unlocked the breechblock from the barrel and allowed it to slide back on its own, extracting and ejecting the spent case, cocking the hammer, and compressing a coiled spring in the rear of the gun. The spring then pushed the breechblock forward, stripping a fresh cartridge from a magazine in the handgrip, and the toggle locked the breechblock once more against the barrel.

Borchardt's toggle and spring mechanisms were improved by a German, Georg Luger, who came up with the 7.65-mm (later 9-mm) Parabellum pistol. This was adopted by the German army in 1908.

In the United States and many parts of Europe, John M. Browning's handgun designs dominated the first half of the 20th century. In his 11.43-mm (.45-inch) pistol, manufactured by Colt and adopted by the U.S. military in 1911, the barrel and breechblock were covered and locked together by a housing called the slide. When the gun was fired, the recoiling slide pulled the barrel back a short distance until the barrel was disengaged and returned to its forward position by a spring. The unlocked slide and breechblock continued back, ejecting the spent case and cocking the hammer, until a spring forced them forward while a fresh cartridge was picked up from a seven-round magazine in the grip. The M1911 Colt did not begin being replaced until 1987. Its successor, the 9-mm (.35-inch) Italian Beretta, given the NATO designation M9, reflected post-1970 trends such as large-capacity magazines (15 shots in the Beretta), double-action triggers (which could snap the hammer without its having to be cocked manually or automatically), and ambidextrous safety levers.

CHAPTER 6

MACHINE GUNS AND SPECIALTY SHOULDER WEAPONS

The search for greater firepower has not been limited to shoulder firearms. In addition to personal-defense weapons, a variety of infantry-support weapons classed as machine guns have been subjected to intense experimentation. In addition, greater firepower has been sought in the ability to fire exploding rounds from shoulder weapons as well as recoilless launchers.

EARLY MANUAL MULTIBARRELED WEAPONS

During the flintlock era a number of heavy guns were developed that could fire several bullets either serially or in volley, but it was not until the mid-19th century, with the spread of centre-fire cartridge ammunition and better manufacturing techniques, that such weapons could be put to effective military use. The best known were the Gatling gun, invented by the American Richard J. Gatling, and the mitrailleuse, produced by the Belgian firm of Christophe & Montigny.

THE GATLING GUN

Gatling guns had several barrels (usually 6 or 10) mounted around a central axle and revolved by means of a hand crank. After a barrel fired a round, it went through successive unlocking, extracting, ejecting, reloading, and relocking. In the most successful Gatling guns, stacks of rounds could be fed by means of a feed device to give

RICHARD J. GATLING

Richard Jordan Gatling was born on Sept. 12, 1818, in Maney's Neck, N.C. His career as an inventor began when he assisted his father in the construction and perfecting of machines for sowing cotton seeds and for thinning cotton plants. In 1839 he perfected a practical screw propeller for steamboats, only to find that a patent had been granted to John Ericsson for a similar invention a few months earlier. He established himself in St. Louis, Mo., in 1844, and, taking the cotton-sowing machine as a basis, he adapted it for sowing rice, wheat, and other grains. The introduction of these machines did much to revolutionize the agricultural system in the country.

Becoming interested in the study of medicine during an attack of smallpox, Gatling completed a course at the Ohio Medical College in 1850. In the same year, he invented a hemp-breaking machine, and in 1857 a steam plow. At the outbreak of the American Civil War he devoted himself at once to the perfecting of firearms. In 1861 he conceived the idea of the rapid-fire machine gun that is associated with his name. By 1862 he had succeeded in building the weapon, which was capable of firing 350 rounds per minute; but the war was practically over before the federal authorities approved its use. In 1866 it was officially adopted by the army, which ordered a hundred. In 1870 Gatling moved to Hartford, Conn., to supervise manufacture of the Gatling gun at the Colt Patent Fire Arms Manufacturing Company. He made several more improvements in the gun, which eventually attained a rate of fire of 1,200 rounds per minute (3,000 when motor-driven), and then sold his patent rights to Colt. In later years Gatling worked on a new method for casting cannon, and he also built a motorized plow. He died on Feb. 26, 1903, in New York City.

continuous fire for long periods. Gatling weapons were made to take a variety of ammunition, up to a 2.5 cm (1 inch) in calibre. A few were used by U.S. forces in Cuba in 1898 and in minor military operations around the world.

THE MITRAILLEUSE

The French mitrailleuse was also a multibarreled weapon, but it used a loading plate that contained a cartridge for each of its 25 barrels. The barrels and the loading plate remained fixed, and a mechanism (operated by a crank) struck individual firing pins simultaneously or in succession. The mitrailleuse issued to the French army fired 11-mm (.433-inch) Chassepot rifle ammunition. Weighing more than 900 kg (2,000 pounds), it was mounted on a wheeled carriage and was usually employed in volley fire, all barrels discharging at once. French forces in the Franco-Prussian War of 1870–71 endeavoured to use it in a manner similar to artillery, but it was no match for breech-loading cannon firing explosive shells.

HEAVY MACHINE GUNS

Self-actuated machine guns, which operate under energy generated by a fired round, became militarily effective after the introduction of nitrocellulose propellants. These burn at a more controlled rate than did the older black-powder propellants, generating pressures that build up over a longer time. The first automatic weapons to take advantage of this were heavy guns firing the new, high-velocity rifle cartridges.

RECOIL

The first successful automatic machine gun was invented by Hiram Stevens Maxim, an American working in Europe. Beginning about 1884, he produced a number of weapons in which the bullet's recoil energy was employed to unlock the breechblock from the barrel, to extract and eject the fired case from the gun, and to store sufficient energy in a main spring to push the bolt forward, pick up a fresh round, load the chamber, and lock the piece. Both barrel and breechblock, locked together, recoiled a short distance to the rear; then the barrel was stopped and the block continued back alone. If the trigger was held in firing position, the weapon would continue to fire until it expended all of its ammunition. Rounds were fed to the gun on

Hiram Maxim showing his grandson how to fire his invention, the automatic machine gun. Hulton Archive/Getty Images

belts, which could be clipped together to provide continuous fire, and overheating was solved by surrounding the barrel in a metal jacket in which water was circulated from a separate container.

Maxim's salesmen provided armies with guns in any calibre, usually matching their current rifle cartridge. In Britain, Maxim guns were first chambered for the 11.43-mm (.45-inch) Martini-Henry cartridge, but, as issued in 1891, they fired the 7.70-mm (.303-inch) smokeless-powder round of the Lee-Metford rifle. During the Russo-Japanese War (1904–05), the

Russians used English-made Maxim guns chambered for their 7.62-mm (.30-inch) Mosin-Nagant round. Their Model 1910 weighed about 72 kg (160 pounds), including mount, water-cooling apparatus, and a protective steel shield for the gunner. The German Model 1908, chambered for the 7.92-mm (.31-inch) Mauser cartridge, weighed 45 kg (100 pounds) with its sled mount. Such light weights, made possible because the cartridge was the sole source of power, allowed these weapons to be operated by special infantry units.

Machine guns of the Maxim type had a destructive power never seen before in warfare. In the 1890s, British infantry units used Maxim guns, fabricated under contract by Vickers Sons, to cut down hordes of poorly armed rebels in Africa and Afghanistan. In World War I, a few of them could cause thousands of casualties. Their defensive fire so limited the offensive power of infantry that the entire Western Front, from the Swiss border to the English Channel, became one vast siege operation.

Gas Operation

Not all the early heavy machine guns were of the recoil-operated Maxim type. Gas operation was also employed. In this system a piston located in a cylinder below the barrel was driven to the rear by gas diverted from the barrel through a port. The piston unlocked the breech-block and sent the bolt back against the main spring; a new round was then picked up, moved into the chamber, and fired on the forward stroke.

The best-known gas-operated heavy machine gun was the Hotchkiss, introduced in France in 1892 and modified several times until the definitive version of 1914. It was air-cooled, but the barrel itself was heavy and provided with metal fins to increase heat radiation. A slower method of feeding ammunition by short strips instead of long belts also helped to keep the weapon from overheating. The Japanese used Hotchkiss guns chambered for their 6.5-mm (.26-inch) round against Russia in 1904–05. In World War I, two French Hotchkiss guns firing 8-mm (.312-inch) Lebel cartridges were said to have fired 75,000 rounds each in the defense of Verdun and to have remained serviceable.

Blowback

A third principle of machine-gun operation was often called blowback. In this, the action and barrel were never locked rigidly together; the barrel did not move, nor was there a gas cylinder and piston. To prevent the breech from opening so early that propellant gases would rupture the spent cartridge case, the block was heavy and the main spring strong. Also, there was usually a linkage of parts not quite on centre to delay the actual opening. Finally, the barrel was shorter than usual, allowing the bullet and gases to leave the barrel quickly.

The Austrian Schwarzlose of 1907/12, firing 8-mm (.312-inch) Mannlicher rounds, operated by delayed blowback. It was entirely satisfactory in combat during World War I.

LIGHT MACHINE GUNS

Heavy machine guns were satisfactory for defensive roles but were not really portable. A number of lighter machine guns (frequently called machine rifles or automatic rifles) began to be used in 1915. These included the British Lewis gun (invented in America but manufactured and improved in Great Britain), the French Chauchat, several German weapons, and the U.S. M1918 Browning automatic rifle (known as the BAR). Most, but not all, of these light weapons were gas-operated. Almost all were air-cooled. Generally, they fired from magazines rather than belts of ammunition because detachable magazines were more convenient and more easily transported. Weighing as little as 7 kg (15 pounds), they were light enough to be carried by one man and fired rifle-fashion or from a prone position.

After World War I, light machine guns virtually took over the functions of their heavier counterparts, although the older weapons continued in service around the world through World War II and for decades thereafter. In Germany, where heavy, water-cooled Maxim-type guns had been forbidden by the victorious Allies, an entirely new generation of light machine guns was introduced by the Maschinengewehr 1934 and 1942. Recoil-operated and fed 7.92-mm (.31-inch) rifle ammunition on belts, these were equally effective when fired from bipods or when mounted on tripods for sustained fire. Firing at an extremely high rate (as high as 1,000 rounds per minute), they dealt with the overheating problem by being built with barrels that could be changed in seconds. The MG34 pioneered the quick-change mechanism, while the MG42, being fabricated largely of stamped sheet-metal parts welded and riveted together, could be made cheaply and quickly even in factories designed for automobile manufacture.

The Soviets began to issue their Degtyarev Pekhotny (DP) in 1933 and supplied it to loyalist forces in the Spanish Civil War. In 1944 it was modified into the DPM. British infantry units fought World War II with the Bren, a 7.70-mm (.303-inch) version of a weapon designed by the Czech weapons maker Václav Holek, and U.S. troops relied on the BAR. All were gas-operated and magazine-fed and weighed from slightly over 9 kg (20 pounds) to more than 13.5 kg (30 pounds) loaded. They fired slowly enough to deliver accurate bursts from their bipods, 350–600 rounds per minute.

After the war, with assault-rifle cartridges becoming standard issue, terms such as automatic rifle, light machine gun, and medium machine gun gave way to general-purpose machine gun (GPMG) and squad automatic weapon

(SAW). Most GPMGs are chambered for intermediate-size 7.62-mm (.30-inch) cartridges, while SAWs fire small-calibre, high-velocity rounds such as the 5.56-mm (.22-inch) NATO or the 5.45-mm (.21-mm) Kalashnikov. Significant belt-fed GPMGs include the West German MG3, a modernized version of the MG42; the Mitrailleuse d'Appui Général (MAG), built by Fabrique Nationale of Belgium; the U.S.-made M60; and the Soviet/Russian Pulemyot Kalashnikova (PK). Of the SAWs, the most prominent are the belt- or magazine-fed Minimi, built by Fabrique Nationale, and the magazine-fed Ruchnoy Pulemyot Kalashnikova (RPK).

LARGE-CALIBRE MACHINE GUNS

With the eclipse of the early water-cooled machine guns, the term *heavy* has been applied to machine guns firing cartridges of several times rifle calibre—most often .50 inch or 12.7 mm.

Even before World War I, fully automatic weapons were used with ammunition more powerful than rifle cartridges, but such ammunition was not necessary for infantry missions until foot soldiers encountered armoured vehicles. During the 1930s, many higher-powered weapons were adopted, although only two had outstanding success. One was the United States' M2 Heavy Barrel Browning. Essentially a 12.7-mm (.50-inch) version of the 7.62-mm (.30-inch)

M1917 Browning (a Maxim-type machine gun produced too late to see much fighting in World War I), the M2 was still widely used throughout the noncommunist world decades after World War II. Its cartridge delivered bullets of various weights and types at high muzzle velocities, with roughly five to seven times the energy of full rifle-power ammunition. The weapon was recoil-operated and air-cooled, and it fired at about 450 rounds per minute. The Soviet 12.7-mm (.50 inch) weapon, the Degtyarov-Shpagin Krupnokaliberny 1938 (DShK-38), was similar, but it was gas-operated. It went into wide use in Soviet-supplied countries. Both of these weapons, as well as their successors (such as the Soviets' Nikitin-Sokolov-Volkov, or NSV, machine gun), were used by infantry units on wheeled or tripod mounts, but they were also mounted on tanks to provide defensive fire against ground vehicles or aircraft.

After 1945, several superheavy machine guns (more than 12.7 mm [.50 inch]) were developed, mostly for antiaircraft use. The single most important was a 14.5-mm (.57-inch) weapon first introduced by the Soviets for use in armoured vehicles. It was recoil-operated and belt-fed and had a barrel that could be changed quickly. Later it was fielded on a variety of wheeled carriages and was known as the Zenitnaya Protivovozdushnaya Ustanovka. The ZPU-4, a four-barreled version towed on a trailer, shot down many U.S. aircraft during that nation's

An American military trainer looks on as a soldier in El Salvador (kneeling, front) practices using a grenade launcher in the 1980s. John Hoagland/Getty Images

involvement in the Vietnam War (1965–73) and remains in service in various parts of the world.

GRENADE LAUNCHERS

Soldiers have always favoured grenades for the killing and stunning effect of their explosive power, but the effectiveness of hand grenades has always been limited to the distance they can be thrown. Extending the range of grenades requires that they be launched by some sort of infantry weapon.

SINGLE SHOT

During World War I, most armies developed attachments for standard service rifles that permitted the launching of "rifle" grenades. However, although range was increased with these devices, accuracy remained poor. An effective answer was a shoulder-fired grenade launcher developed in the 1950s by the Springfield Armory. Resembling a single-shot, break-open, sawed-off shotgun, the M79 lobbed a 40-mm (1.57-inch), 176-gram (6-ounce) high-explosive fragmentation grenade at a velocity of 250 feet per second to a maximum range of 400 yards. This covered the area between the longest range of hand-thrown grenades (27.4 to 36.6 metres [30 to 40 yards]) and the middle range of 60-mm (2.7-inch) mortars (274 to 365 metres [300 to 400 yards]).

The M79 employed a "high-low pressure system" developed by Germany during World War II. This involved an aluminum cartridge case with a sealed propellant chamber in front of the primer. The propellant chamber was perforated by a number of partially completed, carefully sized holes leading into a separate expansion chamber within the cartridge case. Upon firing, the high pressures created inside the propellant chamber flowed into the expansion chamber through the previously prepared holes. The resulting moderated gas pressure produced a low impulse that launched the grenade at an adequate velocity and with an acceptable recoil impulse.

M79 grenade launchers were made from 1961 to 1971 and saw a great deal of action in Vietnam. Production was terminated in favour of a launcher attachment for the M16 rifle.

AUTOMATIC FIRE

Grenade-launching machine guns also appeared during the Vietnam War. Instead of the thin-walled projectiles fired

Two U.S. Marines firing an AT4 light shoulder-mounted antitank weapon. Sgt. Mauricio Campino USMC/U.S. Department of Defense

by the M79, these shot higher-velocity cartridges. The weapons were first mounted on helicopters but afterward appeared on tripods and armoured vehicles. On these mounts, grenade-launching machine guns such as the U.S. Mark 19, firing 40-mm (1.6-inch) rounds, and the Soviet AGS-17, shooting 30-mm (1.2-inch) projectiles, frequently replaced or supplemented 12.7-mm (.50-inch) heavy machine guns.

ANTITANK WEAPONS

Upon their introduction in World War I, tanks posed a very serious problem for foot soldiers. The Germans quickly reacted by introducing the 13-mm (.512-inch) Tankgewehr ("Antitank Rifle"), a very large-scale single-shot version of the Mauser bolt-action rifle. British designers created the magazine-fed, bolt-action .55-inch (14-mm) Boys antitank rifle in the late 1930s, and the Soviets introduced 14.5-mm (.57-inch) bolt-action and self-loading antitank rifles during World War II. The increasing thickness of tank armour soon made all of these infantry weapons obsolete, since kinetic-energy weapons that could penetrate tank armour became too heavy and produced too much recoil to be fired from the shoulder.

The search for a shoulder-fired anti-tank weapon took another turn with the application of a principle discovered in the 1880s by an American inventor, Charles E. Munroe. Munroe found that a hollow cone of explosive material, when detonated with its open end a few inches from metal plate, produced a jet of white-hot gases and molten steel that could penetrate many inches of the best armour. Utilizing the Munroe principle, various "shaped-charge" projectiles were first delivered during World War II by low-velocity, shoulder-held rocket launchers such as the bazooka or by recoilless devices such as the German Panzerfaust ("Tank Fist," or "Tank Puncher"). Issued in the latter half of the war, the German weapon was a 76-cm (30-inch)-long, 44.5-mm (1.75-inch)-diameter tube containing a charge of gunpowder. A 152-mm (6-inch)-diameter bomb, mounted on a stick with collapsible fins, was inserted into the front end, and the weapon, held over the shoulder or under the arm, was fired by a simple firing pin and percussion cap on the outside of the tube. The propellant gases blew a cap off of the rear of the tube, in effect canceling the recoil forces generated by the launching of the bomb, which could be lobbed to ranges of 27 to 90 metres (30 to 100 yards). Its powerful shaped charge of RDX and TNT could penetrate any tank armour.

Following World War II, the Soviet military perfected the Panzerfaust-type recoilless launch mechanism in their Ruchnoy Protivotankovy Granatomet 2 (RPG-2), a "Light Antitank Grenade Launcher" featuring a reusable launcher that lobbed an 82-mm (3-inch) shaped-charge warhead more than 135 metres (150 yards). After 1962, with their RPG-7, they combined recoilless launch with a rocket sustainer to deliver a 2.25-kg (5-pound) warhead to targets beyond 450 metres (500 yards). The Soviet RPGs became powerful weapons in the hands of guerrillas and irregular fighters in conflict against more conventionally armed and heavily armoured forces. As such, they were used by the Viet Cong to destroy U.S. armoured vehicles in Vietnam and by militiamen in the protracted conflicts of the Middle East. The RPG-7 and several variants are still used by the Russian army and by many armed forces around the world.

Other countries have developed small, shoulder-held recoilless launchers firing shaped-charge warheads. Some of them, such as the American AT4, come preloaded and are designed to be discarded after firing.

CHAPTER 7

MODERN ARTILLERY

For three centuries after the perfection of cast-bronze cannons in the 16th century, few improvements were made in artillery pieces or their projectiles. Then, in the second half of the 19th century, there occurred a series of advances so brilliant as to render the artillery in use when the century closed probably 10 times as efficient as that which marked its opening. These remarkable developments took place in every aspect of gunnery: in the pieces, with the successful rifling of cannon bores; in the projectiles, with the adoption of more stable elongated shapes; and in the propellants, with the invention of more powerful and manageable gunpowders.

CANNONS

These advances wrought a further transformation in the ever-changing nomenclature and classification of artillery pieces. Until the adoption of elongated projectiles, ordnance was classified according to the weight of the solid cast-iron ball a piece was bored to fire. But, because cylindrical projectiles weighed more than spheres of the same diameter, designation by weight was abandoned, and the calibre of artillery has come to be measured by the diameter of the bore in inches or millimetres. *Cannon* is the general term for large ordnance. A gun is a cannon designed to fire in a flat trajectory, and a howitzer is a shorter piece designed to throw exploding shells in an arcing trajectory. (A mortar, meanwhile, is a very short piece for firing at elevations of more than 45°.)

RIFLED BORES

In the middle years of the 19th century, smoothbore field artillery was placed at a disadvantage by the adoption of rifled small arms, which meant that infantry weapons could now outrange artillery. It therefore became vital to develop rifling for artillery weapons as well. The advantages of rifling were well known, but the technical difficulties of adapting the principle to heavy weapons were considerable. Several systems were tried. These generally involved lead-coated projectiles that could engage shallow rifling grooves or projectiles fitted with studs that would fit into deeper rifling. None proved adequate.

BREECH LOADING

In 1854 William Armstrong, an English hydraulic engineer, designed an entirely new type of gun. Instead of simply boring out a solid piece of metal, Armstrong forged his barrel from wrought iron (later from steel). He then forged a succession of tubes and, by heating and shrinking, assembled them over the basic barrel so as to strengthen it in the area where the greatest internal pressure occurred. The barrel was rifled with a number of narrow, spiral grooves, and the projectile was elongated and coated with lead. The gun was loaded from the rear, the breech being closed by a "vent-piece" of steel that was dropped into a vertical slot and secured there by a large-diameter screw.

Portrait of British industrialist and engineer William Armstrong, inventor of the first breechloaded guns with rifled barrels. W. & D. Downey/Hulton Archive/ Getty Images

The screw was hollow so as to make it lighter and facilitate loading.

In 1859 the British adopted the Armstrong system for field and naval artillery. During this same period, the Prussians had been testing guns made by Alfred Krupp, and in 1856 they adopted their first Krupp breechloader. This was made of a solid steel forging, bored and then rifled with a few deep grooves, and its breech was closed by a transverse sliding steel wedge. The Krupp projectile had a number of soft metal studs set into its surface, positioned so as to align with the rifling grooves. In both the Armstrong and Krupp guns, obturation—that is, the sealing of the breech against the escape of gas—was performed by a soft metal ring let into the face of the vent piece or wedge. This pressed tightly against the chamber mouth to provide the required seal.

Meanwhile, the French adopted a muzzle-loading system designed by Treuille de Beaulieu, in which the gun had three deep spiral grooves and the projectile had soft metal studs. The gun was loaded from the muzzle by engaging the studs in the grooves before ramming the shell.

Armstrong guns were successful against Maoris in New Zealand and during the Opium Wars in China, but the development of ironclad ships in Europe demanded guns powerful enough to defeat armour, and the Armstrong gun's breech closure was not strong enough to withstand large charges of powder.

Romanian troops preparing a gun designed by Alfred Krupp for battle in the early 20th century. Hulton Archive/Getty Images

Therefore, in 1865 the British adopted a muzzle-loading system similar to that of de Beaulieu, since only this would provide the required power and avoid the complications of sealing the breech.

Through the 1870s guns, particularly coastal-defense and naval guns, became longer so as to extract the utmost power from large charges of gunpowder. This made muzzle loading more difficult and gave a greater incentive to the development of an efficient breech-loading system. Various mechanisms were tried, but the one that supplanted all others was the interrupted screw, devised in France. In this system the rear end of the bore was screw-threaded, and a similarly screwed plug was used to close the gun. In order to avoid having to turn the plug several times before closure was effected, the plug had segments of its thread removed, while the gun breech had matching segments cut away. In this way the screwed segments of the plug could be slipped past smooth segments of the breech, and the plug slid to its full depth. Then the plug could be revolved part of a turn, sufficient for the remaining threads to engage with those in the breech.

In the earliest applications of this system, obturation was provided by a thin metal cup on the face of the breechblock; this entered the gun chamber and was expanded tightly against the walls by the explosion of the charge. In practice, the cup tended to become damaged, leading to leakage of gas and erosion of the chamber. Eventually a system devised by another French officer, Charles Ragon de Bange, became standard. Here the breechblock was in two pieces—a plug screwed with interrupted threads and having a central hole, and a "vent bolt" shaped like a mushroom. The stem of the bolt passed through the centre of the breechblock, and the "mushroom head" sat in front of the block. Between the mushroom head and the block was a pad of resilient material shaped to conform to the chamber mouth. On firing, the mushroom head was forced back, squeezing the pad outward so as to provide a gas-tight seal. This system, refined by a century of experience, became the principal method of obturation used with major-calibre artillery.

The alternative to this system was the sliding breechblock and metallic cartridge case pioneered by Krupp. Here the case expanded under the charge pressure and sealed against the chamber walls. As the pressure dropped, the case contracted slightly and could be withdrawn when the breechblock was opened. This system was embraced first by German gunmakers and later was widely used in all calibres up to 800 mm (about 31 inches). However, during World War II (1939–45), when the Germans were faced with metal shortages that threatened cartridge-case production, they developed a form of "ring obturation" so that bagged charges could be used. In this system an expandable metal ring was set into the face of the sliding breechblock, and its seating was vented in such a manner that some of the propellant gas was able to increase the pressure behind the ring and so force it into tighter contact. As improved in the postwar years, this system was adopted on a number of tank and artillery guns.

GUN CONSTRUCTION

The lasting legacy of the Armstrong gun was the system of building up the gun from successive tubes, or "hoops"; this was retained in the rifled muzzle-loading system of the 1870s and was gradually adopted by other countries. Armstrong's method not only economized on material, by distributing metal in accordance with the pressures to be resisted, but it also strengthened the gun.

An exception to the built-up system was practiced by Krupp. He bored guns from solid steel billets, making the barrels in one piece for all but the very largest calibres. In the mid-19th century it was difficult to produce a flawless billet of steel, and a flawed gun would burst explosively, endangering the gunners. A wrought-iron gun, on the other hand, tended to split progressively, giving the gunners warning of an impending failure. This was enough to warrant the use of wrought iron for many years, until steel production became more reliable.

The next major advance in gun construction came in the 1890s with wire-winding, in which one or more hoops were replaced by steel wire wound tightly around the tube. This gave good compressive strength but no longitudinal strength, and the guns frequently bent.

Beginning in the 1920s, wire-winding was abandoned in favour of "auto-frettaging," in which the gun tube was formed from a billet of steel and then subjected to intense internal pressure. This expanded the interior layers beyond their elastic limit, so that the outer layers of metal compressed the inner in a manner analogous to Armstrong's hoops but in a homogenous piece of metal.

RECOIL CONTROL

Until the 1860s guns were simply allowed to recoil along with their carriages until they stopped moving, and they were then manhandled back into firing position. The first attempt at controlling recoil came with the development of traversing carriages for coastal defenses and fortress guns. These consisted of a platform, pivoted at the front and sometimes carried on wheels at the rear, upon which a wooden gun carriage rested. The surface of the platform sloped upward to the rear, so that when the gun was fired and the carriage slid backward up the platform, the slope and friction absorbed the recoil. After reloading, the carriage was manhandled down the sliding platform, assisted by gravity, until the gun was once more in firing position, or "in battery." To compensate for varying charges and, hence, varying recoil forces, the surface of the slide could be greased or sanded.

Control was improved by an American invention, the "compressor." This consisted of loose plates, fitted at the sides of the carriage and overlapping the sides of the slide, which were tightened against the slide by means of screws. Another arrangement was the placing of a number of metal plates vertically between the sides of the slide and a similar set of plates hanging from the carriage, so that one set interleaved the other. By placing screw pressure on the slide plates, the carriage plates were squeezed between them and thus acted as a brake on the carriage movement.

American designers added to this by adopting a hydraulic buffer, consisting of a cylinder and piston attached to the rear of the slide. The fired gun recoiled until it struck the piston rod, driving the piston into the cylinder against a body of water to absorb the shock. British designers then adapted this by attaching the buffer to the slide and the piston rod to the carriage. As the gun recoiled, it drove the piston through water inside the cylinder; meanwhile, a hole in the piston head permitted the water to flow from one side of the piston to the other, giving controlled resistance to the movement. Return to battery was still performed by manpower and gravity.

The final improvement came with the development of mechanical methods of returning the gun to battery, generally by the use of a spring. When the gun recoiled, it was braked by a hydraulic cylinder and at the same time compressed a spring. As recoil stopped, the spring reasserted itself, and the gun was propelled back into battery. From there it was a short step to using compressed air or nitrogen instead of a spring, and such

"hydropneumatic" recoil-control systems became standard after their introduction by the French in 1897.

CARRIAGES AND MOUNTINGS

In 1850 carriages were broadly of two types. Field pieces were mounted on two-wheeled carriages with solid trails, while fortress artillery was mounted either on the "garrison standing carriage," a box-like structure on four small wheels, or on the platform-and-slide mounting previously described.

COAST GUNS

Coastal-defense artillery was the focus of most design attention in the 1870–95 period, since rapidly improving warships appeared to constitute the principal threat. The first major advance was a "disappearing carriage," in which the gun was mounted at the end of two arms that were hinged to a rotating base. In the firing position, a counterweight or hydraulic press held the arms vertical, so that the gun pointed over the edge of the pit in which the mounting was built. On firing, recoil drove the gun back, causing the arms to pivot and sink the gun into the pit out of sight of the enemy, where it could be reloaded in safety. This type of mounting, in various forms, was widely adopted, but it was gradually realized to be excessively complicated in view of the practical difficulty of a ship's gun being able to hit such a small target at long range. In most countries the disappearing mounting ceased to be built in the 1890s, though many of those already in position continued in use into the 1920s in Europe and into the 1940s in the United States.

In the 1890s the "barbette" mounting for coastal-defense guns became the preferred pattern. Here the mounting was in a shallow pit, protected from enemy fire, but the muzzle and upper shield were permanently in view, firing across a parapet that helped protect the gunners. This type of mounting was made practical by the development of hydraulic recoil control systems, which permitted the mounting to remain stationary while the gun, carried in a cradle, was allowed to recoil under control and then return to battery by spring or pneumatic power. The barbette remained the standard mounting for coastal-defense guns until their virtual disappearance after 1945.

FIELD ARTILLERY

Field carriage design entered a new era with the French 75-mm (3-inch) gun of 1897. This introduced an on-carriage hydropneumatic recoil-control system, a shield to protect the gunners, modern sighting, fixed ammunition, and a quick-acting breech mechanism—thus forming the prototype of what became known as the "quick-firing gun." The idea was quickly taken up in other countries, and, by the outbreak of World War I (1914–18), such weapons were standard in all armies. Mountings for larger guns—up to about 155 mm, or 6 inches, in calibre—simply enlarged this basic design.

Up to World War I, with horses providing the standard motive power, it was necessary to design heavy field artillery so that gun and mounting could be dismantled into components, each of which would be within the hauling capacity of a horse team. The gun then traveled in its various pieces until it was reassembled at the firing point. Steam traction was attempted by the British during the South African War (1899–1902), but it was found that tractors could not take guns into firing position, as their smoke and steam was visible to the enemy. The gradual improvement of the internal combustion engine promised a replacement for the horse, but it saw relatively little application until the middle of World War I—and then only for heavier types of artillery.

The type of carriage developed for very heavy weapons was exemplified by that used for the German 420-mm (16.5-inch) howitzers—collectively known as "Big Bertha"—that were used to reduce the fortresses of Liège, Belg., in 1914. The equipment was split into four units—barrel, mounting with recoil system, carriage, and ground platform—which were carried on four wagons pulled by Daimler-Benz tractors. A fifth wagon carried a simple hoist, which, erected over the gun position, was used to lift the components from their wagons and fit them together. As the Great War continued, heavier howitzers and longer-ranging guns were made so large that they could not be split into convenient loads for road movement. Thus, the railway mounting became a major type for guns and howitzers up to

BIG BERTHA

"Big Bertha" actually was any of several 420-mm (16.5-inch) howitzers that were used by advancing German forces to batter the Belgian forts at Liège and Namur in August 1914, at the start of World War I. The guns were designed and built by the firm of Krupp, Germany's largest armaments manufacturer, in the years before the war for the express purpose of overcoming modern forts built of reinforced concrete. The Big Berthas were the largest and most powerful artillery produced to that time. Each gun propelled a shell weighing 950 kg (2,100 pounds) for a distance of almost 14 km (9 miles). The shells were equipped with delayed-action fuses to explode after having penetrated a fortified target. The gun and its carriage, when fully assembled, weighed about 75 tons and was operated and serviced by a crew of about 280 men.

Big Berthas and Austrian Skoda 305-mm (12-inch) howitzers were brought into action against the complex of Belgian forts around Liège on Aug. 12, 1914. They destroyed most of the forts in the next four days, thereby enabling the German army to sweep westward through southern Belgium on its way to invade northern France. Farther to the west, the forts around the city of Namur were similarly battered into surrender by Big Berthas and Skoda guns on August 21–25.

According to some sources, the nickname for the guns was bestowed by the Krupps in honour of Frau Bertha von Bohlen, head of the family. In popular usage, the name Big Bertha was also applied to the extreme long-range cannons with which the Germans shelled Paris in 1918, but these guns are more properly known collectively as the Paris Gun.

520-mm (20.5-inch) calibre. The heaviest guns could be assembled on large mountings, which in turn could be carried on a number of wheels so as to distribute the load evenly onto a railway track. The most impressive railway gun built during the war was the German 210-mm (8.25-inch) "Paris Gun," which bombarded Paris from a range of 109 km (68 miles) in 1918. Like many other railway guns, the Paris Gun was moved to its firing position by rail but, once in place, was lowered to a prepared ground platform.

Advances in carriage design after 1918 were relatively minor. The first was the general adoption of the split trail, in which two trail legs, opened to roughly 45°, were able to support a gun through a wider angle of traverse. Beginning in the 1960s came the gradual adoption of lightweight materials, culminating in the introduction by the British Vickers firm of a carriage built of titanium, which allowed a 155-mm (6-inch) howitzer to be helicopter-lifted. The 1960s also saw the introduction of auxiliary propulsion. Consisting of small motors that drove the wheels of towed guns, this permitted the gun to be moved from its firing position to a concealed or alternative position without calling up the towing vehicle. Propulsion motors also allowed the adoption of powered loading and ramming devices and powered assistance in opening trail legs and lowering platforms, thereby allowing the size of the crew to be reduced.

FIRE CONTROL

Power and range are not enough to render artillery effective. The weapon must be used accurately and reliably. This is the role of fire control—establishing the coordinates of the target and devising an aiming method that will place the artillery piece's shot on target with reliability.

AZIMUTH AND RANGE

In the 1850s the tactics of artillery were simple: the gun was positioned well to the front and fired across open sights straight at the enemy. The general adoption after the 1880s of long-range rifles firing smokeless-powder rounds rendered this tactic hazardous, and the South African War and Russo-Japanese War (1904–05) brought about a change in policy. Guns had to be concealed from the enemy's view, and a system had to be found that allowed them to be aimed without a direct view of the target. The solution was the adoption of the "goniometric," or "panoramic," sight, which could be revolved in any direction and which was graduated in degrees relative to the axis of the gun bore. The gun's position and that of the target were marked on a map, and the azimuth

(the number of degrees clockwise from due north) between the two was measured. A prominent local feature, or a marker placed some distance from the gun, was then selected as an aiming point, and the azimuth between this and the gun's position was also measured. Subtraction of one from the other produced the angle between a line to the aiming point and a line to the target. If this angle was then set on the goniometric sight and the gun shifted until the sight was laid on the aiming point, then the bore of the gun would be pointed at the target.

Once the azimuth was calculated, the range was arrived at by measuring off the map. This was then converted into an angle by consulting a table, calculated during development of the gun, on which ranges were tabulated against angles of elevation. The angle was then set on an adjustable spirit-level (a clinometer) attached to the elevating portion of the gun. Setting the elevation angle displaced a bubble from the level position, and elevating the gun until the bubble returned to the level position brought the gun bore to the correct elevation angle.

The combination of these two techniques was sufficient to fire a shell that would land close to the target. From there, a forward observer would instruct the gunner to change the azimuth and elevation until the shells struck the target. At this point the remaining guns of the battery, which would have followed the corrections and set them on their own sights, would join in to carry out the bombardment.

PREDICTED FIRE

During World War I it became tactically desirable to bombard an enemy position without alerting opposing forces by ranging shots. This brought about the development of "predicted fire."

While it is possible to determine azimuth and range from a map with accuracy, it is difficult to predict the actual performance of a fired shell. The density and temperature of the air through which the shell passes, the temperature of the propelling charge, any variation in weight of the shell from standard, any variation in the velocity of the shell owing to gradual wear on the gun—these and similar environmental changes can alter the performance of the shell from its theoretical values. Beginning in the 1914–18 period, these phenomena were studied and tables of correction were developed, together with a meteorological service that produced information upon which to base the corrections. This technique of predicted fire was slowly improved and was widely used during World War II, but the corrections were an approximation at best, owing to the simple tabular methods of applying the corrections. It was not until the introduction of computers in the 1960s that it became possible to apply corrections more accurately and more rapidly.

TARGET ACQUISITION

Until the second half of the 20th century, target acquisition—a vital part of

A U.S. soldier demonstrating use of an optical targeting device known as the DemonEye MLRF (Micro-Laser Range Finder). Ethan Mikesell – JHUAPL/ Photo Courtesy of U.S. Army

fire control—was almost entirely visual, relying upon ground observers. This was augmented first by observation balloons and then, in World War II, by light aircraft, the object of both being to obtain better visual command over the battlefield. By the late 20th century, satellite imagery and unmanned aerial vehicles (UAVs), combined with GPS, provided unparalleled means of target acquisition.

In World War I two technical methods of targeting enemy gun positions were adopted—sound ranging and flash spotting. In sound ranging, a number of microphones were used to detect the sound waves of a gun being fired; by measuring the time interval between the passing of sound waves across different microphones, it was possible to determine a number of rays of direction that, when plotted on a map, would intersect at the position of the enemy's gun. Flash spotting relied upon observers noting the azimuth of gun flashes and plotting these so as to obtain intersections. Both methods were highly effective, and sound ranging remained a major means of target acquisition for the rest of the century. Flash spotting fell into disuse after 1945, owing to the general adoption of flashless propellants, but since the late 1970s a new type of artillery spotting has been made possible using infrared sensors to detect the position of a fired gun.

AMMUNITION

In 1850, round solid shot and black powder were standard ammunition for guns, while howitzers fired hollow powder-filled shells ignited by wooden fuzes filled with slow-burning powder. The introduction of rifled ordnance allowed the adoption of elongated projectiles, which, because of their streamlined forms, were much less affected by wind than round balls and, being decidedly heavier than balls of like diameter, ranged much farther. This was the beginning of modern ammunition, which now arrives at its targets with increasing accuracy and destructive power.

PROJECTILE, POWDER, AND FUZE

At first, the changing shape of projectiles did not affect their nature. For example, the shrapnel shell, as introduced in the 1790s by the Englishman Henry Shrapnel, was a spherical shell packed with a small charge of black powder and a number of musket balls. The powder, ignited by a simple fuze, opened the shell over concentrations of enemy troops, and the balls, with velocity imparted by the flying shell, had the effect of musket fire delivered at long range. When rifled artillery came into use, the original Shrapnel design was simply modified to suit the new elongated shells and remained the standard field-artillery projectile, since it was devastating against troops in the open.

Owing to the stabilizing spin imparted them by rifling grooves, elongated projectiles flew much straighter than balls, and they were virtually guaranteed to land point-first. Utilizing this principle, elongated powder-filled shells were fitted at the head with impact fuzes, which ignited the powder charge on striking the target. This in turn led to the adoption of powder-filled shells as anti-personnel projectiles. In naval gunnery, elongated armour-piercing projectiles initially were made of solid cast iron, with the heads chilled during the casting process to make them harder. Eventually, shells were made with a small charge of powder, which exploded by friction at the sudden deceleration of the shell upon impact. This was not an entirely satisfactory arrangement, since the shells generally exploded during their passage through the armour and not after they had penetrated to the vulnerable workings of the ship, but it was even less satisfactory to fit the shells with impact fuzes, which were simply crushed upon impact.

Between 1870 and 1890 much work was done on the development of propellants and explosives. Smokeless powders based on nitrocellulose (called ballistite in France and cordite in Britain) became the standard propellant, and compounds based on picric acid (under various names such as lyddite in Britain, melinite in France, and shimose in Japan) introduced modern high-explosive filling for shells. These more stable compounds demanded the development of fuzes adequate for armour-piercing shells, since friction was no longer a reliable method of igniting them. This was accomplished by fitting fuzes at the base of the shells, where impact against armour would not damage them but the shock of arrival would initiate them.

Time fuzes, designed to burst shrapnel shell over ground forces at a particular point in the shell's trajectory, were gradually refined. These usually consisted of a fixed ring carrying a train of gunpowder, together with a similar but moveable ring. The moveable ring allowed the time of burning to be set by varying the point at which the fixed ring ignited the moveable train and the point at which the moveable train ignited the explosive.

During World War I these fuzes were fitted into antiaircraft shells, but it was discovered that they burned unpredictably at high altitudes. Powder-filled fuzes that worked under these conditions were eventually developed, but the Krupp firm set about developing clockwork fuzes that were not susceptible to atmospheric variations. These clockwork fuzes were also used for long-range shrapnel firing; inevitably, an undamaged specimen was recovered by the British, and the secret was out. By 1939 clockwork fuzes of various patterns, some using spring drive and some centrifugal drive, were in general use.

World War I also saw the development of specialized projectiles to meet various tactical demands. Smoke shells, filled with white phosphorus, were adopted for screening the activities of troops; illuminating shells, containing magnesium flares suspended by parachutes, illuminated the battlefield at night; gas shells, filled with various chemicals such as chlorine or mustard gas, were used against troops; incendiary shells were developed for setting fire to hydrogen-filled zeppelins. High explosives were improved, with TNT (trinitrotoluene) and amatol (a mixture of TNT and ammonium nitrate) becoming standard shell fillings.

World War II saw the general improvement of these shell types, though the same basic features were used and flashless propellants, using nitroguanidine and other organic compounds, gradually took over from the earlier simple nitrocellulose types. The proximity fuze was developed by joint British–American research and was adopted first for air defense and later for ground bombardment. Inside the proximity fuze was a small radio transmitter that sent out a continuous signal; when the signal struck a solid object, it was reflected and detected by the fuze, and the interaction between transmitted and received signals was used to trigger the detonation of the shell. This type of fuze increased the chances of inflicting damage on aircraft targets, and it also allowed field artillery to burst shells in the air at a lethal distance above ground targets without having to establish the exact range for the fuze setting.

Since 1945 the proximity fuze has been improved by the transistor and the integrated circuit. These have allowed fuzes to be considerably reduced in size, and they also have allowed the cost to be reduced, making it economically possible to have a combination proximity/impact fuze that would cater to almost all artillery requirements. Modern electronics also have made possible the development of electronic time fuzes, which, replacing the mechanical clockwork type, can be more easily set and are much more accurate.

NUCLEAR SHELLS, GUIDED PROJECTILES, AND ROCKET ASSISTANCE

Nuclear explosive was adapted to artillery by the United States' "Atomic Annie," a 280-mm (11-inch) gun introduced in 1953. This fired a 15-kiloton atomic projectile to a range of 27 km (17 miles), but, weighing 85 tons, it proved too cumbersome for use in the field and was soon obsolete. In its place, nuclear projectiles with yields ranging from 0.1 to 12 kilotons were developed for conventional 203-mm (8-inch) howitzers. Soviet major-calibre artillery was also provided with nuclear ammunition.

The 1970s saw the first moves toward "improved conventional munitions." These were artillery projectiles carrying a number of subprojectiles—antipersonnel bombs or mines or antitank mines—that could be fired from a gun and would be opened, by a time fuze, over the target area to distribute the submunitions. This increased the destructive power of an artillery shell by a large amount and allowed field artillery to place obstacles in the path of enemy tanks at a range of several miles. A further step was the development of guided projectiles. With the 155-mm (6-inch) Copperhead, a U.S. system, a forward observer could "illuminate" a target with laser light, a portion of which would be reflected and picked up by sensors in the approaching shell. The greater part of the shell's flight would be entirely ballistic, but in the last few hundred yards it would be controlled by fins or other means, which, guided by the laser detection system, would "home" the shell onto the target.

In order to improve the range of guns, rocket-assisted projectiles were developed, with moderate success, by the Germans during World War II, and they were the subject of further development in succeeding years. Rocket assistance had certain drawbacks—notably, the loss of payload space in the shell to the rocket motor. A system designed to solve this problem was "base bleed," in which a small compartment in the base of the shell was filled with a piece of smokeless propellant. This would burn during flight, and the emergent gases would fill the vacuum left behind the shell in its passage through the air, reducing aerodynamic drag on the shell and improving the range by about 25 to 30 percent.

MORTARS

The mortar declined in importance during the 19th century but was restored by World War I, when short-range, high-trajectory weapons were developed to drop bombs into enemy trenches. Early designs in that conflict ranged from the 170-mm (6.7-inch) German Minenwerfer ("mine thrower"), which was almost a scaled-down howitzer, to primitive muzzle-loading devices manufactured from rejected artillery shells. The prototype of the modern mortar was a three-inch weapon developed by the Englishman Wilfred Stokes in 1915. This consisted of a smooth-bored tube, resting upon a baseplate and supported by a bipod, that had a fixed firing pin at its breech end. The bomb was a simple cylinder packed with explosive and fitted with a shotgun cartridge at the rear; its fuze was adapted from a hand grenade. When the bomb was dropped down the barrel of the mortar, it fired automatically as the shotgun cartridge struck the fixed firing pin. The bomb was unstable in flight but sufficiently accurate for its purpose, and it was soon replaced by a teardrop-shaped bomb with fins at the rear, which lent greater stability and accuracy. The Stokes mortar was rapidly adopted or copied by all belligerents.

Some more recent mortars have been built with rifled barrels, since these provide better sealing of the propellant gas and greater stability and accuracy owing to the spin imparted to the bomb. The difficulty here is to arrange for the bomb to be drop-loaded freely and yet engage the rifling once the propelling charge exploded. The U.S.-made M30, a 107-mm (4.2-inch) rifled mortar, uses a saucer-shaped copper disk behind the bomb that flattens out into the rifling under gas pressure and provides obturation. In the 120-mm (4.75-inch) French Hotchkiss-Brandt type, produced by several manufacturers today, a prerifled copper driving band, wrapped around the bomb, expands under gas pressure and engages the grooves in the barrel.

ANTIAIRCRAFT ARTILLERY

The development of artillery fired from the ground in defense against aerial attack began as early as 1910, when the airplane first became an effective weapon. A century later, modern versions of these weapons are still important, providing a last line of defense against aircraft that have penetrated the screen of early-warning radar and antiaircraft missiles.

Heavy Weapons and the Problem of Fire Control

Even in the early years of military aircraft, the manufacture of suitable antiaircraft guns and mountings was not difficult, but the fire-control problem, involving a target moving in three planes at high speed, was almost insoluble. The first fire-control system used complex gun sights that aimed the gun well in front of the target in order to give the shell time to reach it. The first projectiles were shrapnel, since scattered lead balls were sufficient to damage the aircraft of the day.

During World War I, attacks by German zeppelins led the British to produce incendiary shells. Forced to correct fire by visual methods, they fitted the shells with tracer devices, which, by leaving a trail of flame and smoke, indicated the shell's trajectory in the air. The French invented the "central post" system of fire control, in which an observing instrument in the centre of the battery calculated the aiming information, which was then passed on to the guns. This removed complex sights from the weapons and reduced the number of skilled operators required in a battery. Early warning of approaching aircraft was by visual means and acoustic devices.

In the 1920s work began on the design of "predictors," mechanical computers that could be given the course, height, and speed of the aircraft as well as the ballistic constants of the gun and could then calculate the gun data necessary to place the shell in the future position of the aircraft. These represented a significant advance in antiaircraft fire, but they still relied upon raw data provided by visual acquisition and tracking. In World War II, radar brought more accurate and timely acquisition and tracking, and the gradual adoption of electrical, rather than mechanical, predictors produced more accurate fire control. Also, rapid-loading and fuze-setting devices were incorporated into gun mountings so that a high rate of fire could be achieved.

The proximity fuze removed the need for fuze setting and thus speeded up the rate of fire, until it was possible for guns of 90- to 100-mm (3.5- to 4-inch) calibre to fire at rates up to 60 rounds per minute. However, in the 1950s, when all these techniques were perfected, guided surface-to-air missiles became practical, and, in all major countries except for the Soviet Union, the use of medium and heavy air-defense guns ceased.

Light Weapons

Light air-defense guns, of calibres from 20 to 40 mm (roughly from .75 to 1.5 inch), were developed in the 1930s for protection against dive bombers and low-level attack. The most famous of these was a 40-mm gun sold by the Swedish firm of Bofors. Virtually an enlarged machine gun, this fired small exploding shells at a rate of about 120 rounds per minute—fast enough to provide a dense screen

American soldiers practicing using a Bofors antiaircraft gun during World War II. The weapon sprayed a rapid-fire curtain of bullets into the air as planes flew overhead. The Frank S. Errigo Archive/Hulton Archive/Getty Images

of fragments through which the aircraft would have to fly. Fire control was largely visual, though some guns were equipped with predictors and power control.

The advent of lightweight missiles also threatened to render the light gun obsolete in the 1950s, but two decades later

the development of electro-optical sights, using television and thermal-imaging technology and allied to computers and powered mountings, led to a resurgence of this class of weapon, if only as a supplement to surface-to-air missiles. In Egyptian hands in October 1973, the Soviet ZSU-23-4, consisting of four 23-mm (.9-inch) guns mounted on a tracked vehicle, shot down many Israeli fighters over the Sinai Peninsula. Variants of the ZSU-23-4 are still fielded by the Russian army and several other armed forces. The Bofors firm has mounted its guns on wheeled vehicles, and since the 1960s the United States has fielded mobile systems called Vulcan and Phalanx, which consist of a six-barreled, Gatling-type gun firing 20-mm (.75-inch) ammunition.

ANTITANK GUNS

The development of dedicated heavy weapons for attacking tanks began in earnest in the 1930s. These were all in the 20- to 40-mm (.75- to 1.5-inch) class, were mounted on light, two-wheeled, split-trail carriages, and were adequate against the tanks of the day. As tanks acquired heavier armour during World War II, so the guns became larger, eventually reaching 128 mm (5 inches) in calibre. The guns themselves did not generally demand new technology, but the development of ammunition had to break new ground.

The initial antitank projectile was a solid shot of hardened steel, and, in order to penetrate thicker tank armour, it was fired at higher and higher velocities. However, at a striking velocity of about 800 metres (2,600 feet) per second, steel shot shatters upon impact instead of penetrating. In order to overcome this, projectiles of tungsten carbide were used. The Germans designed a gun with a bore actually tapering in diameter from breech to muzzle, and for ammunition they constructed a projectile with a tungsten core and a soft metal body that would deform and squeeze in the reducing bore. The combination of reduced base area and constant gas pressure increased the projectile's velocity, and the "taper-bore" or "squeeze-bore" gun proved formidable. Guns were developed with tapering calibres of 28/20, 41/29, and 75/55 mm (1/1.25, 1.6/1.1, 3/2 inches), but wartime shortages of tungsten led to their abandonment after 1942. In 1944 Britain perfected "discarding-sabot" projectiles, in which a tungsten core is supported in a conventional gun by a light metal sabot that splits and falls free after leaving the muzzle, allowing the core to fly on at extremely high velocity.

An alternative method is to use high explosives in the form of shaped-charge or squash-head projectiles. The shaped charge is an explosive formed into a hollow cone and lined with heavy metal; upon detonation, the explosive gases and molten metal form a high-velocity jet capable of punching through armour. The squash-head shell uses a plastic explosive filling, which, deposited on the armour and then detonated, drives a shock wave through the plate. This results in the failure of the inner face and the ejection of a massive slab of metal into the tank.

Heavy antitank guns relying upon high-velocity projectiles largely fell into disuse after 1945, but the technology has been perpetuated in the main armament mounted on tanks. Explosive-energy projectiles are also used on tanks as well as on recoilless guns.

RECOILLESS GUNS

Military inventors were long attracted by the prospect of abolishing recoil, since achieving this meant doing away with a gun's heavy recoil system and lightening the carriage. The first to succeed was Comdr. Cleland Davis of the U.S. Navy, who in 1912 developed a gun with a single chamber and two opposite barrels. One barrel carried the projectile, the other an equal weight of grease and lead shot. The explosion of the central cartridge ejected both loads, and, since the recoils had the same weight and velocity, they canceled each other out and the gun remained stationary. Davis' idea was adopted in 1915 by the Royal Naval Air Service, which ordered guns of 40, 57, and 75 mm (1.5, 2.25, and 3 inches) for arming aircraft against airships and submarines. Few were made, however, and there appears to be no record of their use in combat.

If the Davis principle were taken to its logical ends, the countershot could be half the weight and twice the velocity of the principal projectile or any other combination giving the same momentum; at its ultimate, the countershot could simply be a cloud of high-velocity gas. This was the system upon which recoilless guns of up to 105 mm (4.1 inches) were developed during World War II. The cartridge cases of these weapons had a weakened section that ruptured on firing, allowing about four-fifths of the propellant gas to be exhausted to the rear of the gun. There they passed through a venturi, a nozzle with a constricted portion that increased the gas velocity and so balanced the recoil generated by the projectile. The back-blast caused by the exhausted gases made these weapons difficult to emplace and conceal, but after 1945 they were universally adopted as light antitank weapons.

CHAPTER 8

TANKS AND OTHER ARMOURED VEHICLES

Tanks are heavily armed and armoured combat vehicles that move on two endless metal chains called tracks. Tanks are the principal type of armoured vehicle. Other major types include tracked and wheeled infantry carriers, and amphibious assault vehicles.

TANKS

Tanks are essentially weapon platforms that make the weapons mounted in them more effective by their cross-country mobility and by the protection they provide for their crews. Weapons mounted in tanks have ranged from single rifle-calibre machine guns to, in recent years, long-barreled guns of 120- or 125-mm (4.75- or 4.92-inch) calibre.

EARLIEST DEVELOPMENTS

The use of vehicles for fighting dates to the 2nd millennium BCE, when horse-drawn war chariots were used in the Middle East by the Egyptians, Hittites, and others as mobile platforms for combat with bows and arrows. The concept of protected vehicles can be traced back through the wheeled siege towers and battering rams of the Middle Ages to similar devices used by the Assyrians in the 9th century BCE. The two ideas began to merge in the battle cars proposed in 1335 by Guido da Vigevano, in 1484 by Leonardo da Vinci, and by others, down to James Cowen, who took out a patent in England in 1855 for an armed, wheeled, armoured vehicle based on the steam tractor.

But it was only at the beginning of the 20th century that armoured fighting vehicles began to take practical form. By then the basis for them had become available with the appearance of the traction engine and the automobile. Thus, the first self-propelled armoured vehicle was built in 1900 in England when John Fowler & Company armoured one of their steam traction engines for hauling supplies in the South African (Boer) War (1899–1902). The first motor vehicle used as a weapon carrier was a powered quadricycle on which F.R. Simms mounted a machine gun in 1899 in England. The inevitable next step was a vehicle that was both armed and armoured. Such a vehicle was constructed to the order of Vickers, Sons and Maxim Ltd. and was exhibited in London in 1902. Two years later a fully armoured car with a turret was built in France by the Société Charron, Girardot et Voigt, and another was built concurrently in Austria by the Austro-Daimler Company.

To complete the evolution of the basic elements of the modern armoured fighting vehicle, it remained only to adopt tracks as an alternative to wheels. This became inevitable with the appearance of the tracked agricultural tractor, but there was no incentive for this until after the outbreak of World War I. A tracked armoured vehicle was proposed in France as early as 1903 but failed to arouse the interest of military authorities, as did a similar proposal made in England in 1908. Three years later a design for a tracked armoured vehicle was rejected by the Austro-Hungarian and then by the German general staffs, and in 1912 the British War Office turned down yet another design.

WORLD WAR I

The outbreak of World War I in 1914 radically changed the situation. Its opening stage of mobile warfare accelerated the development of armoured cars, numbers of which were quickly improvised in Belgium, France, and Britain. The ensuing trench warfare, which ended the usefulness of armoured cars, brought forth new proposals for tracked armoured vehicles. Most of these resulted from attempts to make armoured cars capable of moving off roads, over broken ground, and through barbed wire. The first tracked armoured vehicle was improvised in July 1915, in Britain, by mounting an armoured car body on a Killen-Strait tractor. The vehicle was constructed by the Armoured Car Division of the Royal Naval Air Service, whose ideas, backed by the First Lord of the Admiralty, Winston S. Churchill, resulted in the formation of an Admiralty Landships Committee. A series of experiments by this committee led in September 1915 to the construction of the first tank, called "Little Willie." A second model, called "Big Willie," quickly followed. Designed to cross wide trenches, it was accepted by the British Army, which ordered 100 tanks of this type (called Mark I) in February 1916.

A British tank at the Western Front, World War I. Encyclopædia Britannica, Inc.

Simultaneously but independently, tanks were also developed in France. Like the very first British tank, the first French tank (the Schneider) amounted to an armoured box on a tractor chassis; 400 were ordered in February 1916. But French tanks were not used until April 1917, whereas British tanks were first sent into action on Sept. 15, 1916. Only 49 were available and their success was limited, but on Nov. 20, 1917, 474 British tanks were concentrated at the Battle of Cambrai and achieved a spectacular breakthrough. These tanks, however, were too slow and had too short an operating range to exploit the breakthrough. In consequence, demand grew for a lighter, faster type of tank, and in 1918 the 14-ton Medium A appeared with a speed of 13 km (8 miles) per hour and a range of 130 km (80 miles). After 1918, however, the most widely used tank was the French Renault F.T., a light six-ton vehicle designed for close infantry support.

When World War I ended in 1918, France had produced 3,870 tanks and Britain 2,636. Most French tanks survived into the postwar period; these were the Renault F.T., much more serviceable than their heavier British counterparts. Moreover, the Renault F.T. fitted well with traditional ideas about the primacy of the infantry, and the French army adopted the doctrine that tanks were a mere auxiliary to infantry. France's lead was followed in most other countries; the United States and Italy both assigned tanks to infantry support and copied the Renault F.T. The U.S. copy was the M1917 light tank, and the Italian was the Fiat 3000. The only other country to produce tanks by the end of the war was Germany, which built about 20.

INTERWAR DEVELOPMENTS

The Renault F.T. remained the most numerous tank in the world into the early 1930s. Aware of the need for more

French tanks and soldiers in the streets of Katowice, Pol., during one of the Silesian uprisings, 1919–21. Encyclopædia Britannica, Inc.

powerful vehicles, if only for leading infantry assaults, the French army took the lead in developing well-armed tanks. The original 1918 French Schneider and Saint-Chamond tanks already had 75-mm (3-inch) guns, while the heavier British tanks were at best armed with 57-mm (2.25-inch) guns. After the war the French built 10 68-ton 2C tanks with the first turret-mounted 75-mm guns and continued to develop 75-mm-gun tanks, notably the 30-ton Char B of 1936.

In the meantime, Britain took the lead, technically and tactically, in developing the mobility of tanks. Even before World War I had ended, work had started on the Medium D, with a maximum speed of 32 km (20 miles) per hour. Between 1923 and 1928 the British Army ordered 160 of the new Vickers Medium tanks. They were virtually the only tanks the British Army had until the early 1930s and the only tanks to be produced in quantity anywhere in the world during the mid-1920s. The Vickers Mediums stimulated the Royal Tank Corps to develop mobile tactics, and various experiments during the 1920s and early '30s resulted in the general adoption of two categories of tanks. Mobile tanks were intended for the role performed earlier by horse cavalry, while slower but more heavily armoured tanks provided infantry support.

Before this division into mobile and slow tanks had crystallized, several different designs were tried. The British Independent tank of 1925, with five turrets, started a trend toward multi-turreted heavy tanks. Another trendsetter was a small turretless tankette, originated in Britain by Maj. Giffard le Quesne Martel and John Carden in the mid-1920s, and a slightly heavier, turreted, two-man light tank. The number of light tanks grew rapidly after 1929, as several countries started to produce armoured vehicles. The Soviet Union was by far the most important producer; on a much smaller scale Poland, Czechoslovakia, and Japan entered the field in 1930–31. Concurrently, tank production started up again in France and Italy.

As tank production grew and spread among nations, the value of light tanks armed only with machine guns decreased, and heavier models armed with 37- to 47-mm (1.45- to 1.85-inch) guns for fighting other tanks began to displace them. An early example was the Vickers-Armstrong six-ton model of 1930, copied on a large scale in the Soviet Union (as the T-26). The most successful example was the BT, also built in large numbers in the Soviet Union. The fastest tank of its day, the BT was based on designs evolved in the United States by J.W. Christie, who in 1928 built an experimental model capable of 68 km (42.5 miles) per hour. Christie's vehicles could run on wheels after the removal of tracks and, far more significant, had road wheels independently suspended. This enabled them to move over broken ground faster than tanks with the earlier types of suspension.

Although they were relatively well-armed and mobile, tanks of the T-26 and BT type were lightly armoured (plates with thicknesses of 10 to 15 mm, or 0.4 to 0.6 inch) and were not, therefore, suitable for close infantry support. This was clearly demonstrated in 1937 during the civil war in Spain, where T-26 and BT tanks were used by the Republican forces. Even before this time, it had become clear that tanks that moved at the slow pace of the infantry and were therefore exposed to the full effect of antitank guns had to be thickly armoured. This realization led in the mid-1930s to such infantry tanks as the French R-35 with 40-mm (1.5-inch) armour and the British A.11 with up to 60-mm (2.25-inch) armour.

Apart from being lightly armoured, the Soviet BT, the equivalent British cruiser tanks, and the German Pz. III also required support from more heavily armed tanks if they were to engage in fighting of any intensity. The need for tanks with more powerful 75-mm (3-inch) guns was clearly recognized in Germany, leading in 1934 to the design of the Pz. IV. The problem was realized less clearly in the Soviet Union, even though the T-28 and T-35 multi-turret tanks with 76-mm guns were first built there in 1932–33. But the Russians recognized more quickly than others the need for the next step, which was to replace all the light-medium tanks armed with 37- to 47-mm guns by medium tanks armed with 75- or 76-mm guns. Thus, in 1939, while the Germans were still developing the Pz. III from a 37-mm (1.45-inch) to a 50-mm (2-inch) version, the Russians were already concentrating on the T-34 medium tank with a 76-mm gun.

Other armies were farther behind in producing well-armed tanks on the eve of World War II. All but 80 of the 1,148 tanks that Britain had produced between 1930 and 1939 were still armed only with machine guns. Italy was even worse off, with only 70 M/11 tanks with 37-mm guns while the rest of its total of 1,500 were small, machine-gun-armed tankettes. The United States had only about 300 machine-gun-armed light tanks. Most of the 2,000 tanks produced in Japan were equally lightly armed. By comparison, France had a more powerful tank force—2,677 modern tanks, of which, however, only 172 were the Char B, armed with 75-mm guns. The largest force was the Soviet Union's, which, as a result of a massive production program started in 1930–31, had about 20,000 tanks by 1939, considerably more than the rest of the world put together.

WORLD WAR II

The most effective tank force proved to be the German, composed in 1939 of 3,195 vehicles, including 211 Pz. IVs. What made the German panzers so formidable was that, instead of being divided between various infantry and cavalry tank units, they were all concentrated and used in massed formations in the panzer divisions. The successes of the panzer divisions during the first two years of World War II led the major armies to reorganize most of their tanks into similar formations; this resulted in a dramatic increase in production.

The campaigns of 1939–41, in which armoured forces played an

THE SHERMAN TANK

The M4 General Sherman tank was designed and built by the United States for the conduct of World War II. The most widely used tank series in the war, it was employed not only by the U.S. Army and Marine Corps but also by British, Canadian, and Free French forces. The M4 was employed in North Africa, Sicily, Italy, and western Europe and throughout the Pacific theatre.

The first American main battle tank employed in combat in World War II was the M3 General Grant, named for the American Civil War general Ulysses S. Grant. However, the M3 was only an interim measure. Production ceased in late 1942, when the M4 went into full production. The prototype of the M4, named for Grant's subordinate William Tecumseh Sherman, debuted in 1941 and was accepted for production that October. Its designers consciously emphasized speed and mobility, limiting the thickness of the armour and the size of the main gun, thereby compromising on firepower and survivability. The M4's main armament was a short-barreled, low-velocity 75-mm (3-inch) gun, and its armour thickness was a maximum of 75 mm and a minimum of 12 mm (3 inches and 0.5 inch). The tank had a maximum speed of 38 to 46 km (24 to 29 miles) per hour and a range of 160 to 240 km (100 to 150 miles), depending on the series. The M4 carried a crew of five—commander, gunner, loader, driver, and codriver/hull gunner. A typical power plant was a 425-horsepower gasoline engine.

The M4 entered active service with the British in North Africa in October 1942. It was roughly in the same class as early versions of the German Pz. IV. Later-model German tanks were much improved, so that by the time of the Normandy Invasion in June 1944 the M4 was outclassed by superior tanks such as the Pz. V (Panther) and the Pz. VI (Tiger). The American penchant for mass production tended to stymie innovations in technology, and American doctrinal thinking tended to remain stuck in the prewar period, when the tank was seen as primarily an infantry support weapon. As a result, the M4 was not "up-gunned" until late in the war, and American, British, and Canadian tank crews consistently faced better German tanks. The M4 had a faster rate of fire and greater speed, but both the Panther and the Tiger had significantly greater range and accuracy. The German tanks were also more survivable. Consequently, it took superior numbers for Anglo-American forces to defeat German armoured formations. The most notable effort to break the Germans' qualitative advantage was the Firefly, a Sherman equipped with a 76.2-mm long-barreled gun (a "17-pounder").

For the Normandy Invasion and subsequent campaigns on the Continent, the M4 was retrofitted with special-purpose devices by both the Americans and the British. The British added flails (a system of rotors and chains) to clear paths through minefields, and American servicemen added jury-rigged plows for breaking through hedgerows. Perhaps the most famous variation was the "Duplex Drive," or DD, tank, a Sherman equipped with extendable and collapsible skirts that made it buoyant enough (at least in theory) to be launched from a landing craft and make its way to shore under propeller power. Numerous devices of all sorts were fitted onto the Sherman's versatile, reliable chassis, making it the workhorse of the Anglo-American armies of World War II. A total of 49,324 Sherman tanks were produced in 11 plants between 1942 and 1946.

important role, also intensified the technical development of tanks and other armoured vehicles. The German Pz. IV and Soviet T-34 were rearmed in 1942 with longer-barreled, higher-velocity guns; soon afterward these began to be displaced by more powerfully armed tanks. In 1943 the Germans introduced the Panther medium tank with a long 75-mm (3-inch) gun having a muzzle velocity of 936 metres (3,070 feet) per second, compared with 384 metres (1,260 feet) per second for the original Pz. IV and 750 metres (2,460 feet) per second for its 1942 version. The 43-ton Panther weighed almost twice as much as its predecessor and was correspondingly better armoured. Germany also introduced the still more powerful Tiger tank, armed with an 88-mm (3.5-inch) gun. Its final version (Tiger II), at 68 tons, was to be the heaviest tank used during World War II. To oppose it, the Russians brought out the JS, or Stalin, heavy tank, which appeared in 1944 armed with a 122-mm (4.8-inch) gun. Its muzzle velocity was lower than that of the German 88-mm guns, however, and it weighed only 46 tons. At about the same time the T-34 was rearmed with an 85-mm (3.3-inch) gun.

In contrast to the breakthrough role of the earlier heavy tanks, the Tiger and JS tanks functioned chiefly to support basic medium tanks by destroying enemy tanks at long range. German and Soviet armies also developed other heavy vehicles for this purpose, such as the Jagdtiger, with a 128-mm (5-inch)

gun, and the ISU, with a 122-mm (4.8-inch) gun; these, in effect, were turretless tanks. In addition, all armies developed lightly armoured self-propelled antitank guns. The U.S. Army developed a specialized category of tank destroyers that resembled self-propelled guns in being relatively lightly armoured but that, like tanks, had rotating turrets.

The turretless-tank type of vehicle originated with the Sturmgeschutz, or assault gun, introduced by the German army for infantry support but subsequently transformed into more versatile vehicles particularly suited for destroying enemy tanks. No such vehicles were produced in Britain or the United States. Throughout the war, however, the British Army retained a specialized category of infantry tanks, such as the Churchill, and of cruiser tanks, such as the Crusader and Cromwell. The former were well-armoured and the latter were fast, but none was well-armed compared with German and Soviet tanks. As a result, during 1943 and 1944 British armoured divisions were mostly equipped with U.S.-built M4 Sherman medium tanks.

The M4 was preceded by the mechanically similar M3 General Grant medium tank. Like the M4, the M3 also was armed with a medium-velocity 75-mm (3-inch) gun but had it mounted in the hull instead of the turret. Given this configuration, the M3 could be put into production more quickly when tanks were urgently required in 1940 and 1941.

A U.S. M3 General Grant tank on a training exercise during World War II, 1942. Library of Congress, Washington, D.C.

Production of the M4 began in 1942. Successful when first introduced, it was by 1944 no longer adequately armed and should have been replaced by a new medium tank. But the U.S. Army, like the British, adhered to the fallacious doctrine that armoured divisions should confine themselves to exploitation of infantry breakthroughs and did not, therefore, need powerfully armed tanks. Only toward the end of the war did the U.S. Army introduce a few M26 Pershing heavy tanks with a 90-mm (3.5-inch) gun comparable to that of the original German Tiger. Similarly, the British Army introduced the prototypes of the Centurion tank with a 76-mm (3-inch) gun comparable to that of the German Panther. Otherwise, U.S. and British tanks were well behind the German and Soviet tanks in their gun power.

POSTWAR TANK DEVELOPMENT

After World War II it was generally recognized that all tanks must be well-armed to fight enemy tanks. This finally ended the division of tanks into under-gunned categories of specialized infantry and cavalry tanks, which the British Army retained longer than any other. Still not fully recognized, however, were the advantages of concentrating tanks in fully mechanized formations, and the British and U.S. armies continued to divide tanks between the armoured divisions and the less mobile infantry divisions. After World War II, tanks also suffered from one of the periodic waves of pessimism about their future. New antitank weapons, such as rocket launchers and recoilless rifles, and the mistaken belief that the value of tanks lay primarily in their armour protection caused this attitude. The Soviet army, however, maintained large armoured forces, and the threat they posed to western Europe as the Cold War became more intense, together with the havoc created by Soviet-built T-34/85 tanks during the North Korean invasion of South Korea in 1950, provided a new impetus to development.

The development of tactical nuclear weapons in the mid-1950s provided further stimulus to the development of tanks and other armoured vehicles. Nuclear weapons encouraged the use of armoured forces because of the latter's mobility and high combat power in relation to their vulnerable manpower. Moreover, armoured vehicles proved capable of operating in relative proximity to nuclear explosions by virtue of their protection against blasts and radioactivity.

As less emphasis was placed after a time on nuclear weapons and more on conventional forces, tanks retained their importance. This was based on their being recognized, particularly from the early 1970s, as the most effective counter to other armoured forces, which formed the principal threat posed on the ground by potential aggressors.

ARMAMENT

In keeping with the importance attached to the ability of tanks to defeat enemy tanks, great emphasis was placed after World War II on their armament. The result was progressive increases in the calibre of tank guns, the development of new types of ammunition with greater armour-piercing capabilities, and the introduction of more sophisticated fire-control systems to improve tank guns' ability to hit targets.

Gun Calibre

Increases in gun calibre are well illustrated by the British Centurion, which started in 1945 with a 76-mm (3-inch) gun but in 1948 was rearmed with an 83.8-mm (3.3-inch) gun and in 1959 with an even more powerful 105-mm (4.1-inch) gun. Moreover, during the 1950s the capabilities of British tank units were augmented by a small number of Conqueror heavy tanks armed with 120-mm (4.75-inch) guns, and in the early 1970s the Centurions were entirely replaced by

Chieftains armed with new and more-effective 120-mm guns.

Similar increases took place in the calibre of Soviet tank guns. After World War II the basic T-34/85 tanks armed with 85-mm (3.35-inch) guns were replaced by T-54 and T-55 tanks armed with 100-mm (4-inch) guns. They were followed in the 1960s by the T-62, with a 115-mm (4.5-inch) gun, and in the 1970s and '80s by the T-64, T-72, and T-80, all with 125-mm (5-inch) smoothbore guns. The JS-3 and T-10 heavy tanks with their less powerful 122-mm (4.8-inch) guns had by then been withdrawn. This left the Soviet army in the same position as others of having a single type of battle tank as well-armed as contemporary technology would allow.

For a time the U.S. Army also subscribed to a policy of developing heavy as well as medium tanks. But the heavy M103 tank, armed with a 120-mm gun, was only built in small numbers in the early 1950s. As a result, virtually the only battle tanks the U.S. Army had were the M46, M47, and M48 medium tanks, all armed with 90-mm (3.5-inch) guns. After the mid-1950s the M47 tanks were passed on to the French, Italian, Belgian, West German, Greek, Spanish, and Turkish armies, and during the 1960s the M48 began to be replaced by the M60, which was armed with a U.S.-made version of the 105-mm (4.1-inch) gun developed for the British Centurion.

The same 105-mm gun was adopted for the Pz. 61 and Pz. 68 tanks produced in Switzerland, the West German Leopard 1, the Swedish S-tank, the Japanese Type 74, and the Mark 1 and 2 versions of the Israeli Merkava. It was also retained in the original version of the U.S. M1 Abrams tank developed in the 1970s, but the subsequent M1A1 version of the 1980s was rearmed with a 120-mm (4.75-inch) gun originally developed in West Germany for the Leopard 2 tank. The British Challenger, introduced in the 1980s, was also armed with 120-mm (4.75-inch) guns, but these were still of the rifle type.

Ammunition

The last years of World War II saw the development of more-effective antitank ammunition with armour-piercing, discarding-sabot (APDS) projectiles. These had a smaller-calibre, hard tungsten carbide core inside a light casing. The casing fell away on leaving the gun barrel, while the core flew on at an extremely high velocity. The APDS, which was adopted for the 83.8-mm (3.3-inch) gun of the Centurions, was fired with a velocity of 1,430 metres (4,692 feet) per second. By comparison, earlier full-calibre, armour-piercing projectiles had a maximum muzzle velocity of about 900 metres (3,000 feet) per second. With this shell the Centurion's 83.8-mm gun could penetrate armour twice as thick as could the 88-mm (3.5-inch) gun of the German Tiger II of World War II.

An alternative type of armour-piercing ammunition developed during the 1950s was the high-explosive antitank (HEAT) shell. This shell used a shaped

U.S. Army M60 Patton tank, armed with a gun/launcher for firing a 152-mm (5.9-inch) projectile or launching an antitank missile, 1965. U.S. Army Photograph

charge with a conical cavity that concentrated its explosive energy into a very high-velocity jet capable of piercing thick armour. The HEAT round was favoured by the U.S. Army for its 90-mm (3.5-inch) tank guns and also by the French army for the 105-mm (4.1-inch) gun of its AMX-30 tank, introduced in the mid-1960s. However, during the 1970s both APDS and HEAT began to be superseded by armour-piercing, fin-stabilized, discarding-sabot (APFSDS) ammunition. These projectiles had long-rod penetrator cores of tungsten alloy or depleted uranium; they could be fired with muzzle velocities

of 1,650 metres (5,400 feet) per second or more, making them capable of perforating much thicker armour than all earlier types of ammunition.

During the 1960s, attempts were made to arm tanks with guided-missile launchers. These were to provide tanks with a combination of the armour-piercing capabilities of large shaped-charge warheads with the high accuracy at long range of guided missiles. The U.S. M60A2 and the U.S.-West German MBT-70 were armed with 152-mm (5.9-inch) gun/launchers firing standard ammunition as well as launching Shillelagh guided antitank missiles, and the AMX-30 was armed experimentally with the 142-mm (5.6-inch) ACRA gun/launcher. But the high cost, unreliability, and slow rate of fire of the missiles, together with the appearance of APFSDS ammunition and greatly improved fire-control systems, led to abandonment of gun/launchers in the early 1970s.

Fire Control

The first major postwar advance in fire-control systems was the adoption of optical range finders, first on the M47 tank and then on the Leopard 1, the AMX-30, and other tanks. In the 1960s, optical range finders began to be replaced by laser range finders. In combination with electronic ballistic computers, these greatly increased the hit probability of tank guns. They became standard in all new tanks built from the early 1970s and were retrofitted in many of the earlier tanks.

Another major development was that of night sights, which enabled tanks to fight in the dark as well as in daylight. Originally of the active infrared type, they were first adopted on a large scale on Soviet tanks. Other tanks were fitted from the 1960s with image-intensifier sights and from the 1970s with thermal imaging sights. These latter were called passive because, unlike active infrared systems, they did not emit energy and were not detectable.

After World War II an increasing number of tanks were fitted with stabilized gun controls to enable them to fire more accurately on the move (i.e., to keep their gun barrels at a constant angle of elevation even while the tank was riding over bumps or depressions). At first some tanks, such as the T-54, had their guns stabilized only in elevation, but the Centurion already had stabilization in traverse as well as elevation, and this became standard beginning in the 1970s. Afterward tanks were also provided with independently stabilized gunners', as well as commanders', sights, the better to engage targets on the move.

ARMOUR

Until the 1960s, tank armour consisted of homogeneous steel plates or castings. The thickness of this armour varied from 8 mm (0.3 inch) on early tanks to 250 mm (10 inches) at the front of the German Jagdtiger of 1945. After World War II, opinions differed about the value of armour protection. Tanks such as the Leopard 1 and AMX-30 had relatively thin armour for the sake of light weight and greater mobility, which was considered to provide a greater chance of battlefield survival. Other tanks, such as the Chieftain, had heavier armour, up to 120 mm (4.75 inches) thick at the front, and the Arab-Israeli wars of 1967 and 1973 demonstrated the continued value of heavy armour.

At the same time, new types of armour were developed that were much more effective than homogeneous steel, particularly against shaped-charge warheads.

The new types were multilayered and incorporated ceramics or other nonmetallic materials as well as steel. The first was successfully developed in Britain under the name of Chobham armour. Armour of its kind was first adopted in the early 1970s in the M1 and Leopard 2; it then came into general use in place of simple steel armour.

Fighting in Lebanon in 1982 saw the first use, on Israeli tanks, of explosive reactive armour, which consisted of a layer of explosive sandwiched between two relatively thin steel plates. Designed to explode outward and thus neutralize the explosive penetration of a shaped-charge warhead, reactive armour augmented any protection already provided by steel or composite armour.

The increased protection afforded to tanks inevitably increased their weight. Some tanks introduced during the 1950s and '60s, such as the T-54 and AMX-30, weighed only 36 tons, but the Chieftain already weighed 54 tons. Most tanks introduced during the 1980s, such as the M1 and the Leopard 2, also weighed more than 50 tons, and the Challenger weighed as much as 62 tons.

MOBILITY

In spite of the progressive increases in weight, tanks' speed and agility actually increased because they were provided with more powerful engines. After World War II, tank engines had an output of 500 to 800 horsepower, but, starting with the MBT-70, their output increased to 1,500 horsepower. Engines of this power were installed in the M1 and the Leopard 2, giving them power-to-weight ratios of more than 20 horsepower per ton.

Most tank engines of the immediate postwar years had 12 cylinders in a V-configuration and at first were of the spark-ignition gasoline type. But Soviet tanks already had diesel engines, and from the 1960s almost all tanks were diesel-powered. This increased their range of operation because of the greater thermal efficiency of the diesels, and it reduced the risk of catastrophic fires that could erupt if the armour was perforated by enemy weapons.

The development of gas turbines led in the 1960s to the use of one, in combination with a diesel engine, in the Swedish S-tank. After that, a 1,500-horsepower gas turbine was adopted to power by itself the M1 and M1A1. A gas turbine also powered the Soviet T-80, introduced in the 1980s. All other new tanks of the 1980s and after continued to be powered by diesels because of their greater fuel economy.

Since the speed of tanks over rough ground depended not only on the power of their engines but also on the effectiveness of their suspensions, the latter developed considerably in the postwar era. Almost all tanks adopted independently located road wheels, sprung in most cases by transversely located torsion bars. Exceptions to this were the Centurion and Chieftain and the

Merkava, which used coil springs. To improve their ride over rough ground still further, most tanks built from the 1980s were fitted with hydropneumatic instead of metallic spring units.

CONFIGURATION

The great majority of postwar tanks continued the traditional configuration of driver's station at the front of the hull, engine compartment at the rear, and rotating turret at the centre. The turret mounted the main armament and was occupied by the tank's commander, gunner, and loader. This configuration, introduced by the Vickers-Armstrong A.10 tank designed in 1934, became almost universal after World War II, but after 1960 it was abandoned in some cases in favour of novel configurations. One widely adopted configuration retained the turret but replaced the human loader by an automatic loading mechanism. The first examples of this were on the T-64 and T-72 tanks, whose guns were automatically loaded from a carousel-type magazine below the turret. Another tank with an unconventional configuration was the Merkava, which had its engine compartment at the front and the ammunition at the rear of the hull, where it was least likely to be hit by enemy fire. The Merkava also had a turret with a low frontal area, which reduced the target it presented to enemy weapons.

OTHER ARMOURED VEHICLES

Although the tank is the principal fighting armoured vehicle, other types of military vehicles are fitted with offensive weaponry as well as partial or complete armour plating for protection against bullets, shell fragments, and other projectiles. These vehicles move either on wheels or, like tanks, on continuous tracks. They include armoured personnel carriers, infantry fighting vehicles, and other vehicles such as amphibious assault vehicles that are designed primarily as platforms for assault troops.

ARMOURED PERSONNEL CARRIERS

Armoured personnel carriers (APCs) are tracked armoured vehicles that are used for transporting infantry into battle. APCs first appeared in large numbers early in World War II, when the German army adopted them to carry the infantry contingents of their panzer and panzer grenadier divisions into battle. After World War II, improvements to APCs made them even more capable of accompanying tanks into battle.

HALF-TRACKED CARRIERS

Though a few experimental armoured carriers were built in Britain at the end of World War I, development did not really flourish until the Germans adopted them to carry infantry in their panzer divisions at the beginning of World War II. Germany's example was quickly followed by the United States, which by the end of the war had produced some 41,000 carriers. Both the German and U.S. carriers of World War II were of the half-tracked type, which combined two standard wheels on the front axle with a rear propulsion system based on caterpillar tracks. In the German army the most effective vehicles were in the SdKfz (Sonderkraftfahrzeug, or "Special Motor Vehicle") series. The SdKfz 251, built with armour 6 to 14.5 mm (0.25 to 0.57 inch) thick and armed with two mounted machine guns, could carry 10 men into battle.

The American equivalent was the Carrier, Personnel, Half-Track M3. These vehicles provided only minimal protection. Nevertheless, they represented a major advance over the earlier method of transporting infantry into battle in unarmoured trucks. Moreover, German panzer grenadiers used them effectively as combat vehicles and fought from them on the move, thus greatly increasing the mobility of infantry on the battlefield.

FULLY TRACKED CARRIERS

In the postwar era the U.S. Army led the development of fully tracked infantry carriers with all-around armour protection. The first postwar carrier was the large M44, which had a crew of 2 and could carry 25 soldiers. This was followed in 1952 by the M75, which had a similar box body but carried only 12 soldiers. The U.S. Army used a few M75s successfully during the Korean War.

In 1955 the M75 began to be replaced by the M59, which was similar in appearance but was less expensive and could swim across calm inland waters. In 1960 the U.S. Army fielded the M113, which had a lower silhouette and was considerably lighter. The M113 was the first aluminum-armoured vehicle to be put into large-scale production. After its appearance, several other armoured carriers, light tanks, and self-propelled guns were built with aluminum armour. Within 30 years the United States had produced more than 76,000 M113 APCs and their derivatives, making them the most numerous armoured vehicles outside the Soviet bloc. M113 carriers were used extensively in the Vietnam War, often as combat vehicles, although they were not designed for that role and were at a disadvantage in spite of the addition of roof-mounted machine guns with protective shields. Although they have been superseded as infantry carriers by newer models, M113s continue to be used in a variety of roles—for example, for medical evacuation and as mortar carriers.

The British equivalent of the M113 was the FV430 series of tracked vehicles, introduced to the British Army in the 1960s. The FV430 vehicles were made in many versions, including mobile command posts and ambulances. The APC version, the FV432, had a crew of two and could transport eight fully armed soldiers. It was generally armed with a 7.62-mm

(.30-inch) machine gun mounted on the roof. During Britain's combat involvement in the Iraq War (2003–09), a certain number of FV430s were upgraded to a Mark 3, or "Bulldog," configuration, fitted with metal cages and with reactive armour that exploded outward to provide better protection against improvised explosive devices and rocket-propelled grenades.

AMPHIBIOUS ASSAULT VEHICLES

Amphibious assault vehicles (AAVs) are armed and armoured military vehicles designed to deliver assault troops and their equipment from ship to shore under combat conditions. As developed most fully by the United States Marine Corps, AAVs are tracked vehicles that transport troops and materiel over water and continue to function ashore under hostile fire as logistical vehicles or as fighting vehicles.

The origin of modern AAVs can be traced to the 1920s and '30s, when Marine Corps planners, preparing for eventual war in the Pacific against the Japanese empire, considered the central problem posed by amphibious landings from the open seas—specifically, how to deliver assault troops to a defended shore quickly and with sufficient force to establish a secure beachhead and continue fighting inland. To help solve the problem the Marine Corps turned to the Alligator, an amphibious rescue vehicle first built in 1935 by Donald Roebling, a scion of the engineering family founded by John Augustus Roebling. Roebling's lightweight aluminum vehicle

was propelled in water and driven on land by a set of tracks equipped with paddle-like cleats. From this civilian prototype the Marine Corps developed a more powerful steel-plated military version called the Landing Vehicle Tracked, or LVT. Originally built in 1941 as an unarmoured cargo carrier called the amphibian tractor, or amtrac, the LVT quickly acquired armour. Two types evolved: an armoured amphibious personnel and cargo carrier and a turreted amphibious gun-vehicle for close fire support during landing operations. Altogether 18,620 LVTs were built during World War II; these played a prominent role in the Pacific campaigns from Guadalcanal onward.

After World War II, LVTs were successfully used in Korea, notably for the 1950 Inchon landing. Two new models were built between 1951 and 1957: an LVTP-5 amphibious carrier, capable of carrying as many as 37 men, and an LVTH-6 armed with a turret-mounted 105-mm (4.1-inch) howitzer. They were followed in 1972 by the 22.8-ton LVTP-7, which incorporated several improvements, the most important being a boatlike hull with a stern loading ramp instead of a bow ramp and two water-jet propulsion units that greatly improved its performance in comparison with that of the earlier LVTs. At the same time, the LVTP-7 retained the seagoing qualities of the earlier LVTs, which could negotiate rough seas and Pacific surf—in contrast to other amphibious vehicles, which were intended primarily for crossing inland water obstacles.

U.S. Marines conducting exercises with AAVP7A1 amphibious assault vehicles. Courtesy of United States Marine Corps

In 1985 the LVTP-7 was redesignated the AAVP7A1, as part of its continued evolution from a landing vehicle into an assault vehicle. The AAVP7A1 is still an important platform in the U.S. Marine Corps' traditional role as an amphibious force, though it also has been used in conflicts far from the sea, notably in the Iraq War. The vehicle, weighing more than 25 tons fully loaded, can transport 25 combat-ready marines over water at 13 km (8 miles) per hour. On land it can travel over roads at 70 km (45 miles) per hour. Its standard armament consists of a 12.7-mm (.50-inch) machine gun and a 40-mm (1.5-inch) grenade launcher. The AAVP7A1 and its LVTP-7 predecessor have been exported for service in marine forces of other countries—for example, South Korea and Taiwan.

After 2003 Britain's Royal Marines employed the Viking, an amphibious armoured all-terrain vehicle based on a Swedish design. The Viking consists of two tracked units, or cabins, linked by a steering mechanism. The forward cabin, carrying the engine and driver, can transport three fully equipped marines, and the rear cabin has room for eight marines. The sole weapon is a 12.7- or 7.62-mm (.50- or .30-inch) machine gun mounted on the forward cabin. With such a configuration and armament, the Viking is intended to serve primarily as a transport or patrol vehicle and not as an assault platform. It has seen service in Afghanistan.

INFANTRY FIGHTING VEHICLES

The French AMX-VCI of 1958 represented the first attempt to produce a true infantry fighting vehicle (IFV)—that is, a tracked armoured carrier from which infantry could fight effectively. A further step in this direction was taken by the West German army with the HS-30, which included a turret with a 20-mm (.75-inch) cannon. The West German Marder and the Soviet BMP-1, which first appeared in the late 1960s, represented the most significant advances in IFVs since World War II. Both vehicles enabled mounted infantry effectively to engage even armoured opponents—a capability lacking in previous designs. The

Marder weighs 29.2 tons, has a three-man crew, can carry seven infantrymen, and is armed with a turret-mounted 20-mm autocannon. The BMP-1 weighs 13.5 tons, has a three-man crew, can carry eight infantrymen, and is armed with a turret-mounted 73-mm (2.9-inch) gun. A later version, the BMP-2, introduced in the early 1980s, is armed with a high-velocity 30-mm (1.18-inch) cannon; both versions carry externally mounted antitank guided missiles. The BMP-3, in service with the Russian army since the late 1980s and also sold for export, has a 100-mm (4-inch) combined gun and missile launcher and can carry a squad of seven infantrymen.

In the 1980s the U.S. Army introduced the M2 Bradley Infantry Fighting Vehicle. The Bradley weighs 27.6 tons, has a three-man crew, can carry six infantrymen, and is armed with a turret-mounted 25-mm (1-inch) cannon and an antitank missile launcher. The most modern version, the M2A3, includes infrared sights, a laser

An M2 Bradley infantry fighting vehicle during a training exercise at a U.S. military base in Kuwait. Pfc. Khori Johnson/U.S. Army

range finder, and bolt-on reactive armour tiles. Its British equivalent is the Warrior Mechanized Combat Vehicle, introduced in 1986. The Warrior weighs 24.5 tons, has a three-man crew, can carry seven infantrymen, and is armed with a turret-mounted 30-mm (1.18-inch) cannon.

WHEELED ARMOURED VEHICLES

Many countries have also developed wheeled armoured carriers to serve in a variety of roles, including infantry transport, reconnaissance, antitank defense, fire support, engineering, command and control, and medical evacuation. Wheeled vehicles generally have advantages over tracked vehicles in improved on-road performance, better fuel economy, and lower maintenance costs. They are therefore particularly useful in the type of peacekeeping and counterinsurgency operations that have grown more prevalent since the end of the Cold War.

U.S. soldiers in a Stryker wheeled infantry carrier at the Yakima Training Center, Washington. Courtesy of U.S. Army

The Soviet army introduced the first of a successful line of wheeled armoured vehicles, the BTR-60, in the early 1960s. In a typical configuration the BTR-60 weighs 10.1 tons, has a two-man crew, can carry 12 infantrymen, and is armed with a 12.7-mm (.5-inch) heavy machine gun. The Soviets introduced improved versions in the late 1970s (BTR-70) and late 1980s (BTR-80). These latter versions included a turret-mounted 14.5-mm (.57-inch) heavy machine gun and improved power plants, but troop capacity was reduced in order to accommodate these improvements. The Soviets used the BTR vehicles extensively in the Afghan War from 1979 to 1989.

Beginning in 1983, the U.S. Marine Corps fielded the LAV-25, a wheeled light armoured vehicle with all-terrain capabilities. The LAV-25 weighs 12.8 tons, has a three-man crew, can carry six infantrymen, and is armed with a turret-mounted 25-mm (1-inch) chain gun and two 7.62-mm (.30-inch) machine guns.

For roughly two decades the LAV-25 was the only significant U.S. wheeled armoured vehicle program, but in the late 1990s the desire for more rapidly deployable forces convinced the U.S. Army to develop a wheeled armoured vehicle capable of transport by aircraft such as the C130 Hercules. To speed the development process, the Army stressed the use of off-the-shelf technology. The result was the Stryker Infantry Carrier Vehicle (ICV), first fielded in 2003. The Stryker is largely modeled after the Canadian LAV III,

A mine-resistant, ambush-protected all-terrain vehicle (M-ATV), built specifically for mountainous terrain, parked next to a larger armoured vehicle, Kandahar, Afghanistan, 2009. Courtesy of U.S. Army. Photo by Spc. Elisabet Freeburg

which began service with the Canadian Army in 1999 and, in turn, is based on the Swiss Piranha III. The Stryker weighs 18 tons, has a two-man crew, can carry nine infantrymen, and in its primary variant is armed with an M2 .50-inch (12.7-mm) heavy machine gun or a 40-mm (1.5-inch) automatic grenade launcher housed in a remotely operated turret. The U.S. Army has equipped more than a half dozen of its combat brigades with Stryker ICVs, which have seen service in both the Iraq War and the Afghanistan War.

The wars in Iraq and Afghanistan quickly demonstrated the vulnerability of lightly armoured vehicles to mines, rocket-propelled grenades, and improvised explosive devices (IEDs). The U.S. Army responded at first with improvisations, such as adding metal caging around the exterior of Stryker vehicles to cause incoming warheads to detonate prematurely, and by adding armour to its fleet of High Mobility, Multipurpose Wheeled Vehicles (HMMWVs, or Humvees). These adjustments failed to protect against the most lethal IEDs, especially those buried in roadways that attack the underside of a vehicle. To combat these threats, the U.S. Army and Marine Corps fielded thousands of Mine-Resistant, Ambush-Protected

(MRAP) wheeled armoured vehicles. MRAPs are designed with a V-shaped hull to deflect explosions upward and away from the troop compartment. They proved to be twice as effective in safeguarding passengers as M1 Abrams tanks and more than three times as effective as the armoured Humvees. There are a number of variants of the MRAP, including an urban operations vehicle that carries seven soldiers, a troop carrier that can transport 11 soldiers, and other models designed to clear mines and explosives. In general, MRAPs are designed not as combat vehicles but rather as troop carriers.

The weight of MRAPs (with models ranging from 9 to 25 tons) and their top-heavy weight distribution make the vehicles prone to rollovers and less than ideal for off-road use. To improve cross-country performance for environments such as Afghanistan, in 2009 the United States designed and began to field lighter (12-ton) MRAP all-terrain vehicles, or M-ATVs. M-ATVs can carry four soldiers plus a gunner who can man a top-mounted machine gun or grenade launcher.

As the changing battlefield creates new and more lethal threats, the configuration of armoured vehicles will continue to be adjusted accordingly.

CHAPTER 9

ROCKET AND MISSILE SYSTEMS

Rocket and missile systems are any of a variety of weapons systems that deliver explosive warheads to their targets by means of rocket engines. A rocket engine is a self-contained (i.e., non-air-breathing) propulsion system in which the elements of its propulsive jet (that is, the fuel and oxidizer) are self-contained within the vehicle. For the purposes of this book, the term *rocket* refers to any free-flight (unguided) missile of the types used since the beginning of rocketry. Broadly defined, a guided missile is any military missile that is capable of being guided or directed to a target after having been launched. Tactical guided missiles are shorter-ranged weapons designed for use in the immediate combat arena.

MILITARY ROCKETS

There is no reliable early history of the "invention" of rockets. Most historians of rocketry trace the development to China, a land noted in ancient times for its fireworks displays. In 1232, when the Mongols laid siege to the city of Kaifeng, capital of Honan province, the Chinese defenders used weapons that were described as "arrows of flying fire." There is no explicit statement that these arrows were rockets, but some students have concluded that they were because the record does not mention bows or other means of shooting the arrows. In the same battle, it is reported, the defenders dropped from the walls of the city a kind of bomb described as "heaven-shaking thunder." From these meagre references some students have concluded that by 1232 the Chinese had discovered black powder (gunpowder) and had learned to use it to make explosive bombs as well as propulsive charges for rockets. Drawings made in military documents much later show powder rockets tied to arrows and spears. The propulsive jet evidently added to the range of these weapons and acted as an incendiary agent against targets.

In the same century rockets appeared in Europe. There is indication that their first use was by the Mongols in the Battle of Legnica in 1241. The Arabs are reported to have used rockets on the Iberian Peninsula in 1249; and in 1288 Valencia was attacked by rockets. In Italy, rockets are said to have been used by the Paduans (1379) and by the Venetians (1380).

There are no details of the construction of these rockets, but they were presumably quite crude. The tubular rocket cases were probably many layers of tightly wrapped paper, coated with shellac. The propulsive charge was the basic black powder mixture of finely ground carbon (charcoal), potassium nitrate (saltpetre), and sulfur. The English scientist Roger Bacon wrote formulas for black powder about 1248 in his *Epistola*. In Germany a contemporary of Bacon, Albertus Magnus, described powder charge formulas for rockets in his book *De mirabilibus mundi*. The first firearms appeared about 1325; they used a closed tube and black powder to propel a ball, somewhat erratically, over varying distances. Military engineers then began to invent and refine designs for both guns and rockets.

By 1668, military rockets had increased in size and performance. In that year, a German colonel designed a rocket, weighing 60 kg (132 pounds), that was constructed of wood and wrapped in glue-soaked sailcloth. It carried a gunpowder charge weighing 7.25 kg (16 pounds). Nevertheless, the use of rockets seems to have waned, and for the next 100 years their employment in military campaigns appears to have been sporadic.

THE CONGREVE ROCKET

A revival commenced late in the 18th century in India. There Hyder Ali, prince of Mysore, developed war rockets with an important change: the use of metal cylinders to contain the combustion powder. Although the hammered soft iron he used was crude, the bursting strength of the container of black powder was much higher than the earlier paper construction. Thus a greater internal pressure was possible, with a resultant greater thrust of the propulsive jet. The rocket body was lashed with leather thongs to a long bamboo stick. Range was perhaps slightly more than a kilometre. Although individually these rockets were not accurate, dispersion error became less important when large numbers were fired rapidly in mass attacks. They were particularly effective against cavalry and were hurled into the air, after lighting, or skimmed along the hard dry ground. Hyder Ali's son, Tippu Sultan, continued to develop and expand the use of rocket weapons, reportedly increasing the number of rocket troops from 1,200 to a corps of 5,000. In battles at Seringapatam in 1792 and 1799 these rockets were used with considerable effect against the British.

The news of the successful use of rockets spread through Europe. In England Sir William Congreve began to experiment privately. First, he experimented with a number of black-powder formulas and set down standard specifications of composition. He also standardized construction details and used improved production techniques. Also, his designs made it possible to choose either an explosive (ball charge) or incendiary warhead. The explosive warhead was separately ignited and could be timed by trimming the fuse length before launching. Thus, air bursts of the warheads were feasible at different ranges.

Congreve's metal rocket bodies were equipped on one side with two or three thin metal loops into which a long guide stick was inserted and crimped firm. Weights of eight different sizes of these rockets ranged up to 27 kg (60 pounds). Launching was from collapsible A-frame

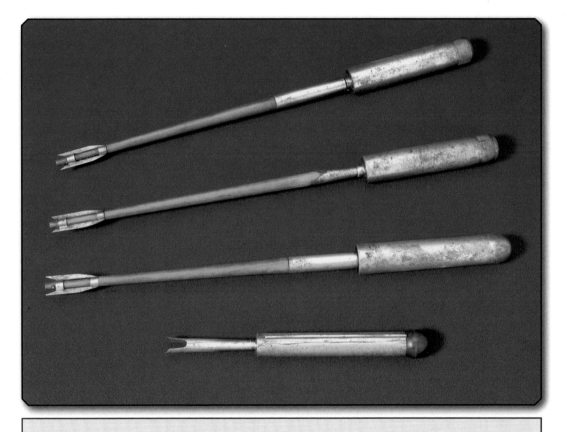

Models of Congreve military rockets. The British made good use of these stick-mounted rockets during several early 19th century battles, including the War of 1812. SSPL via Getty Images

FRANCIS SCOTT KEY AND "THE STAR SPANGLED BANNER"

Francis Scott Key was born on Aug. 1, 1779, on his father's estate in Frederick County, Md. After attending St. John's College and training for the law in Annapolis, he established a success- ful law practice, first in Frederick and then in Washington, D.C. In September 1814, after the burning of Washington by the British during the War of 1812, Key was sent to the British fleet in Chesapeake Bay to secure the release of his friend William Beanes, who had been captured after the defeat of the U.S. forces at Bladensburg, Md. He was detained aboard ship during the shelling of Ft. McHenry, one of the forts that defended Baltimore. During the night of the bombardment, September 13–14, Key's anxiety was at high pitch, and in the morning when he saw the American flag still flying over the fortress, he wrote "The Star-Spangled Banner." Returning to shore that day, he rewrote the poem in a Baltimore hotel. It was printed anony- mously under the title "Defence of Fort M'Henry" and on September 20 was published by the Baltimore Patriot. Set to the tune of an English drinking song, "To Anacreon in Heaven," it soon became popular throughout the nation. It was later adopted by the army and navy as the national anthem, and in 1931 it was officially adopted by Congress. Key continued his law practice in Washington, was U.S. attorney for the District of Columbia from 1833 to 1841, and died on Jan. 11, 1843, in Baltimore.

ladders. In addition to aerial bombard- ment, Congreve's rockets were often fired horizontally along the ground.

These side-stick-mounted rockets were employed in a successful naval bom- bardment of the French coastal city of Boulogne in 1806. The next year a massed attack, using hundreds of rockets, burned most of Copenhagen to the ground. During the War of 1812 between the United States and the British, rockets were employed on numerous occasions. The two best- known engagements occurred in 1814. At the Battle of Bladensburg (August 24) the use of rockets assisted British forces to turn the flank of the American troops defending Washington, D.C. As a result, the British were able to capture the city. In

September the British forces attempted to capture Fort McHenry, which guarded Baltimore harbour. Rockets were fired from a specially designed ship, the *Erebus*, and from small boats. The British were unsuccessful in their bombardment, but on that occasion Francis Scott Key, inspired by the sight of the night engage- ment, wrote "The Star Spangled Banner," later adopted as the United States national anthem. "The rockets' red glare" has continued to memorialize Congreve's rockets ever since.

In 1815 Congreve further improved his designs by mounting his guide stick along the central axis. The rocket's propul- sive jet issued through five equally spaced holes rather than a single orifice. The forward portion of the guide stick, which screwed into the rocket, was sheathed with brass to prevent burning. The centre-stick-mounted rockets were significantly more accurate. Also, their design permitted launching from thin copper tubes.

Maximum ranges of Congreve rockets were from .8–3.2 km (.5–2 miles), depending upon size. They were competitive in performance and cost with the ponderous 10-inch (250-mm) mortar and were vastly more mobile.

The next significant development in rocketry occurred about the middle of the 19th century. William Hale, a British engineer, invented a method of successfully eliminating the deadweight of the flight-stabilizing guide stick. By designing jet vents at an angle, he was able to spin the rocket. He developed various designs, including curved vanes that were acted upon by the rocket jet. These rockets, stabilized by means of spin, represented a major improvement in performance and ease of handling.

Even the new rockets, however, could not compete with the greatly improved artillery with rifled bores. The rocket corps of most European armies were dissolved, though rockets were still used in swampy or mountainous areas that were difficult for the much heavier mortars and guns. The Austrian Rocket Corps, using Hale rockets, won a number of engagements in mountainous terrain in Hungary and Italy. Other successful uses were by the Dutch colonial services in Celebes and by Russia in a number of engagements in the Turkistan War.

Hale sold his patent rights to the United States in time for some 2,000 rockets to be made for the Mexican War, 1846–48. Although some were fired, they were not particularly successful. Rockets were used in a limited way in the American Civil War (1861–65), but reports are fragmentary, and apparently they were not decisive. The U.S. Ordnance Manual of 1862 lists 7.25-kg (16-pound) Hale rockets with a range of 2 km (1.25 miles).

In Sweden about the turn of the century, Wilhelm Unge invented a device described as an "aerial torpedo." Based upon the stickless Hale rocket, it incorporated a number of design improvements. One of these was a rocket motor nozzle that caused the gas flow to converge and then diverge. Another was the use of smokeless powder based on nitroglycerin. Unge believed that his aerial torpedoes would be valuable as surface-to-air weapons against dirigibles. Velocity and range were increased, and about 1909 the Krupp armament firm of Germany purchased the patents and a number of rockets for further experimentation.

ROCKETRY RESEARCH AND EXPERIMENTATION

In the United States, meanwhile, Robert Hutchings Goddard was conducting theoretical and experimental research on rocket motors at Worcester, Mass. Using a steel motor with a tapered nozzle, he achieved greatly improved thrust and efficiency. During World War I Goddard developed a number of designs of small military rockets to be launched from a lightweight hand launcher. By switching from black powder to double-base powder (40 percent nitroglycerin, 60 percent nitrocellulose), a far more potent propulsion charge was obtained. These rockets were proving successful under tests by the U.S. Army when the Armistice was signed; they became the forerunners of the bazooka of World War II.

World War I actually saw little use of rocket weapons, despite successful French incendiary antiballoon rockets and a German trench-war technique by which a grappling hook was thrown over enemy barbed wire by a rocket with a line attached.

Many researchers besides Goddard used the wartime interest in rockets to push experimentation, the most noteworthy being Elmer Sperry and his son, Lawrence, in the United States. The Sperrys worked on a concept of an "aerial torpedo," a pilotless airplane, carrying an explosive charge, that would utilize gyroscopic, automatic control to fly to a preselected target. Numerous flight attempts were made in 1917, some successful. Because of early interest in military use, the U.S. Army Signal Corps organized a separate program under Charles F. Kettering in Dayton, Ohio, late in 1918. The Kettering design used a gyroscope for lateral control to a preset direction and an aneroid barometer for pitch (fore and aft) control to maintain a preset altitude. A high angle of dihedral (upward tilt) in the biplane

wings provided stability about the roll axis. The aircraft was rail-launched. Distance to target was determined by the number of revolutions of a propeller. When the predetermined number of revolutions had occurred, the wings of the airplane were dropped off and the aircraft carrying the bomb load dropped on the target.

The limited time available to attack the formidable design problems of these systems doomed the programs, and they never became operational.

As World War II approached, minor and varied experimental and research activities on rockets and guided missiles were underway in a number of countries. But in Germany, under great secrecy, the effort was concentrated. Successful flights as high as one mile were made in 1931–32 with gasoline–oxygen-powered rockets by the German Rocket Society. Funds for such amateur activities were scarce, and the society sought support from the German army. The work of Wernher von Braun, a member of the society, attracted the attention of Captain Walter R. Dornberger. Von Braun became the technical leader of a small group developing liquid-propellant rockets for the German army. By 1937 the Dornberger–Braun team, expanded to hundreds of scientists, engineers, and technicians, moved its operations from Kummersdorf to Peenemünde, a deserted area on the Baltic coast. Here the technology for a long-range ballistic missile was developed and tested.

BARRAGE ROCKETS

World War II saw the expenditure of immense resources and talent for the development of rocket-propelled weapons. The Germans began the war with a lead in this category of weapon, and their 150-mm and 210-mm (6-inch and 8.25-inch) bombardment rockets were highly effective. These were fired from a variety of towed and vehicle-mounted multitube launchers, from launching rails on the sides of armoured personnel carriers, and, for massive bombardments, even from their packing crates. Mobile German rocket batteries were able to lay down heavy and unexpected concentrations of fire on Allied positions. The 150-mm Nebelwerfer, a towed six-tube launcher, was particularly respected by U.S. and British troops, to whom it was known as the "Screaming Meemie" or "Moaning Minnie" for the eerie sound made by the incoming rockets. Maximum range was more than 5,500 metres (6,000 yards).

A 5-inch (125-mm) rocket with an explosive warhead was developed in Great Britain. Its range was roughly 3–5 km (2–3 miles). These rockets, fired from specially equipped naval vessels, were used in heavy coastal bombardment prior to landings in the Mediterranean. Firing rates were 800–1,000 in less than 45 seconds from each ship.

A development of the U.S. Army was the Calliope, a 60-tube launching projector for 4.5-inch (115-mm) rockets mounted on a Sherman tank. The launcher was mounted on the tank's gun turret, and both azimuth (horizontal direction) and elevation were controllable. Rockets were fired in rapid succession (ripple-fired) to keep the rockets from interfering with one another as they would in salvo firing.

Other conventional rockets developed in the United States included a 4.5-inch (115-mm) barrage rocket with a range of 1,100 yards (1,000 metres) and a 5-inch (125-mm) rocket of longer range. The latter was used extensively in the Pacific theatre of war, fired from launching barges against shore installations, particularly just before landing operations. The firing rate of these flat-bottom boats was 500 per minute. Other rockets were used for smoke laying and demolition. The United States produced more than four million of the 4.5-inch rockets during the war.

Soviet rocket development during World War II was more limited, but extensive use was made of barrage, ripple-fired rockets. Both A-frame and truck-mounted launchers were used. The Soviets mass-produced a 130-mm (5.1-inch) rocket known as the Katyusha. From 16 to 48 Katyushas were fired from a boxlike launcher known as the Stalin Organ, mounted on a gun carriage.

After the war many ground forces continued to field truck-mounted, tube-launched rockets that could be fired simultaneously in salvos or ripple-fired in rapid succession. Such artillery rocket systems, or multiple-launch rocket systems (MLRSs), generally fired rockets of

100 to 150 mm (4 to 6 inches) in diameter and had ranges of 20 to 30 km (12 to 18 miles). The rockets carried a variety of warheads, including high explosive, antipersonnel, incendiary, and smoke. Modernized versions of the Soviet Katyushas saw service in Warsaw Pact armies, and they have been used by regular armies and militias in several conflicts in the Middle East. The U.S. M270 MLRS, mounting 12 rockets on a mobile launcher adapted from a tracked armoured personnel carrier, was used to great effect in the Persian Gulf War of 1990–91.

BAZOOKAS AND PANZERSCHRECKS

Early in World War II, Clarence N. Hickman, who had worked with Robert Goddard during World War I, supervised thse development of a refined design of a hand-launched rocket. The new weapon consisted of a smooth-bore steel tube, originally about 5 feet (1.5 metres) long, open at both ends and equipped with a hand grip, a shoulder rest, a trigger mechanism, and sights. Officially titled the M9A1 Rocket Launcher, it was called "bazooka" after a crude horn of that name used by radio comedian Bob Burns.

The bazooka was developed chiefly for attacking tanks and fortified positions at short range. It launched a 1.6-kg (3.5-pound) rocket with a diameter of 60 mm (2.36 inches) and a length of 48 cm (19 inches). The rocket carried 225 grams (8 ounces) of pentolite, a powerful explosive that could penetrate as much as 125 mm (5 inches) of armour plate. To escape backblast, the operator held the bazooka on his shoulder with about half the tube protruding behind him. The bazooka surprised the Germans when it was first used in the North African landings of 1942. Although the rocket traveled slowly, its potent shaped-charge warhead gave infantrymen the striking power of light artillery.

During the Korean War the M20 "Super Bazooka" was used. This was an aluminum tube that launched a 89-mm (3.5-inch), 4-kg (9-pound) rocket carrying 0.9 kg (2 pounds) of combined RDX/TNT explosive. The chief defects of both bazookas were their cumbersome weight and length and their short effective range (about 120 yards [110 metres]). For this reason, beginning in the Vietnam War the U.S. Army abandoned bazookas in favour of light antitank weapons, or LAWs, such as the M72, a one-shot disposable weapon that weighed 2.3 kg (5 pounds) fully loaded yet could launch its rocket with reasonable accuracy out to 320 metres (350 yards).

The German counterpart of the bazooka during World War II was a light 88-mm (3.5-inch) rocket launcher known as Panzerschreck ("Tank Terror") or Ofenrohr ("Stovepipe"). The Panzerschreck consisted of a lightweight steel tube about 1.5 metres (5 feet) long that weighed about 9 kg (20 pounds). Like the bazooka, the tube was open at both ends and was fitted with a hand grip, a trigger mechanism, and sights. The tube launched a 3.3-kg (7.25-pound)

A 1940s demonstration of the bazooka rocket launcher at Fort Benning, Ga. Hand-held rocket launchers were first used by the U.S. Army in 1942, against German troops in North Africa. © AP Images

rocket-propelled grenade. After loading the rocket in the tube and aiming the weapon at the target, the operator successively pulled two firing triggers, the first to cock the tube's ignition system and the second to fire it, thereby generating a small electrical current that ignited the rocket's motor. The operator was protected from the rocket's backblast by holding the tube on his shoulder with about half the tube protruding behind him. The rocket's low speed in flight meant that the Panzerschreck's maximum

effective range was about 150 metres (500 feet). The rocket carried a powerful hollow-charge explosive that could penetrate 210 mm (8.25 inches) of armour, thicker than that of any Allied tank.

The Panzerschreck was first used by Germany in 1943. The United States claimed that the Germans had copied the design of the bazooka, which had been supplied to the Soviet Red Army in 1942 and had fallen into German hands. In any case, the bazooka certainly stimulated the Germans in their own efforts to design a similar weapon. The Panzerschreck was widely issued to German infantry units and was one of their two main handheld antitank weapons, the other being the Panzerfaust recoilless weapon.

ANTIAIRCRAFT ROCKETS AND AERIAL ROCKETS IN WORLD WAR II

During World War II high-altitude bombing above the range of antiaircraft guns necessitated the development of rocket-powered weapons. In Great Britain, initial effort was aimed at achieving the equivalent destructive power of the 3-inch (75-mm) and later the 3.7-inch (94-mm) antiaircraft gun. Two important innovations were introduced by the British in connection with the three-inch rocket. One was a rocket-propelled aerial-defense system. A parachute and wire device was rocketed aloft, trailing a wire that unwound at high speed from a bobbin on the ground with the object of snagging the aircraft's propellers or shearing off the wings. Altitudes as high as 6,000 metres (20,000 feet) were attained. The other device was a type of proximity fuze using a photoelectric cell and thermionic amplifier. A change in light intensity on the photocell caused by light reflected from a nearby airplane (projected on the cell by means of a lens) triggered the explosive shell.

The only significant antiaircraft rocket development by the Germans was the Taifun. A slender, 1.8 metres (6-foot), liquid-propellant rocket of simple concept, the Taifun was intended for altitudes of 15,000 metres (50,000 feet). The design embodied coaxial tankage of nitric acid and a mixture of organic fuels, but the weapon never became operational.

Britain, Germany, the Soviet Union, Japan, and the United States all developed airborne rockets for use against surface as well as aerial targets. These were almost invariably fin-stabilized because of the effective aerodynamic forces when launched at speeds of 400 km (250 miles) per hour and more. Tube launchers were used at first, but later straight-rail or zero-length launchers, located under the wings of the airplane, were employed. One of the most successful of the German rockets was the 50-mm (2-inch) R4M. The tail fins remained folded until launch, facilitating close loading arrangements. The United States achieved great success with a 114-mm (4.5-inch) rocket, three or four of which were carried under each wing of a fighter plane. These rockets were highly effective against motor columns, tanks, troop and supply trains, fuel and ammunition depots, airfields, and barges.

A variation on the airborne rocket was the addition of rocket motors and fins to conventional bombs. This had the effect of flattening the trajectory, extending the range, and increasing velocity at impact, useful against concrete bunkers and hardened targets. These weapons were called glide bombs, and the Japanese had 100-kg and 370-kg (225-pound and 815-pound) versions. The Soviet Union employed 25- and 100-kg

(55- and 220-pound) versions, launched from the IL-2 Stormovik attack aircraft.

TACTICAL GUIDED MISSILES

Although unguided military rockets still play a role on the modern battlefield, they have yielded in importance to guided missiles, which can be directed to their targets with an accuracy that would have astonished military planners of the mid-20th century. Guided tactical missiles achieve their accuracy by exploiting the entire range of electronic invention that has changed the world since World War II.

GUIDANCE METHODS

The earliest guided missiles used simple command guidance, but within 20 years of World War II virtually all guidance systems contained autopilots or autostabilization systems, frequently in combination with memory circuits and sophisticated navigation sensors and computers. Five basic guidance methods have come to be used: command, inertial, active, semiactive, and passive. Any of these methods can be used alone or in combination with the others. In addition, the various terminal guidance methods are frequently used in combination with global positioning system (GPS) signals to provide even greater accuracy.

COMMAND

Command guidance involves tracking the projectile from the launch site or platform and transmitting commands by radio, radar, or laser impulses or along thin wires or optical fibres. Tracking may be accomplished by radar or optical instruments from the launch site or by radar or video imagery relayed from the missile. The earliest command-guided air-to-surface and antitank munitions were tracked by eye and controlled by hand; later the naked eye gave way to enhanced optics and television tracking, which often operates in the infrared range and issues commands generated automatically by computerized fire-control systems. Another early command guidance method was beam riding, in which the missile sensed a radar beam pointed at the target and automatically corrected back to it. Laser beams were later used for the same purpose. Also using a form of command guidance are television-guided missiles, in which a small camera mounted in the nose of the weapon beams a picture of the target back to an operator who sends commands to keep the target centred in the tracking screen until impact. A form of command guidance used since the 1980s by the U.S. Patriot surface-to-air system is called track-via-missile. In this system a radar unit in the missile tracks the target and transmits relative bearing and velocity information to the launch site, where control systems compute the optimal trajectory for intercepting the target and send appropriate commands back to the missile.

INERTIAL

Inertial guidance was installed in long-range ballistic missiles in the 1950s, but, with advances in miniaturized circuitry, microcomputers, and inertial sensors, it has been common in tactical weapons since the 1970s. Inertial systems involve the use of small, highly accurate gyroscopic platforms to continuously determine the position of the missile in space. These provide inputs to guidance computers, which use the position information in addition to inputs from accelerometers or integrating circuits to calculate velocity and direction. The guidance computer, which is programmed with the desired flight path, then generates commands to maintain the course.

An advantage of inertial guidance is that it requires no electronic emissions from the missile or launch platform that can be picked up by the enemy. Some missiles, therefore, use inertial guidance to reach the general vicinity of their targets and then active radar guidance for terminal homing. Passive-homing antiradiation missiles, designed to destroy radar installations, generally combine inertial guidance with memory-equipped autopilots to maintain their trajectory toward the target in case the radar stops transmitting.

ACTIVE

With active guidance, the missile will track its target by means of emissions that it generates itself. Active guidance is commonly used for terminal homing. Examples are surface-to-air, missiles that use self-contained radar systems to track their targets. Active guidance has the disadvantage of depending on emissions that can be tracked, jammed, or tricked by decoys.

SEMIACTIVE

Semiactive guidance involves illuminating or designating the target with energy emitted from a source other than the missile; a seeker in the projectile that is sensitive to the reflected energy then homes onto the target. Like active guidance, semiactive guidance is commonly used for terminal homing. In the U.S. Hawk and Soviet SA-6 Gainful antiaircraft systems, for example, the missile homes in on radar emissions transmitted from the launch site and reflects off the target, measuring the Doppler shift in the reflected emissions to assist in computing the intercept trajectory. Laser-guided missiles also can use semiactive methods by illuminating the target with a small spot of laser light and homing onto that precise light frequency through a seeker head in the missile.

With semiactive homing the designator or illuminator may be remote from the launch platform. The U.S. Hellfire antitank missile, for example, uses laser designation by an air or ground observer who can be situated far from the launching helicopter.

PASSIVE

Passive guidance systems neither emit energy nor receive commands from an external source; rather, they "lock" onto an electronic emission coming from the target itself. The earliest successful passive homing munitions were "heat-seeking" air-to-air missiles that homed onto the infrared emissions of jet engine exhausts. Among the most advanced passive homing systems are optically tracking munitions that can "see" a visual or infrared image in much the same way as the human eye does, memorize it by means of computer logic, and home onto it. Many passive homing systems require target identification and lock-on by a human operator prior to launch. With infrared antiaircraft missiles, a successful lock-on is indicated by an audible tone in the operator's headset; with television or imaging infrared systems, the operator acquires the target on a screen, which relays data from the missile's seeker head, and then locks on manually.

Passive guidance systems have benefited enormously from a miniaturization of electronic components and from advances in seeker-head technology. Small, heat-seeking, shoulder-fired antiaircraft missiles first became a major factor in land warfare during the final stages of the Vietnam War, with the Soviet SA-7 Grail playing a major role in neutralizing the South Vietnamese Air Force in the final communist offensive in 1975. Ten years later the U.S. Stinger and British Blowpipe proved effective against Soviet aircraft and helicopters in Afghanistan, as did the U.S. Redeye in Central America.

GUIDED-MISSILE SYSTEMS

The principal categories of tactical guided missiles described here are antitank and assault, air-to-surface, and surface-to-air. Distinctions between these categories were not always clear, the launching of both antitank and infantry antiaircraft missiles from helicopters being a case in point.

ANTITANK AND GUIDED ASSAULT

One of the most important categories of guided missile to emerge after World War II was the antitank, or antiarmour, missile. The guided assault missile, for use against bunkers and structures, was closely related. A logical extension of unguided infantry antitank weapons carrying shaped-charge warheads for penetrating armour, guided antitank missiles acquired considerably more range and power than their shoulder-fired predecessors. While originally intended for issue to infantry formations for self-protection, the tactical flexibility and utility of guided antitank missiles led to their installation on light trucks, on armoured personnel carriers, and, most important, on antitank helicopters.

The first guided antitank missiles were controlled by electronic commands transmitted along extremely thin wires played out from a spool on the rear of the missile. Propelled by solid-fuel sustainer rockets, these missiles used aerodynamic fins for lift and control. Tracking was visual, by means of a flare in the missile's tail, and guidance commands were generated by a hand-operated joystick. In operating these missiles, the gunner simply superimposed the tracking flare on the target and waited for impact. The missiles were typically designed to be fired from their carrying containers, with the total package small enough to be carried by one or two men. Germany was developing weapons of this kind at the end of World War II and may have fired some in battle.

After the war French engineers adapted the German technology and developed the SS-10/SS-11 family of missiles. The SS-11 was adopted by the United States as an interim helicopter-fired antitank missile pending the development of the TOW (for tube-launched, optically tracked, wire-guided) missile. Because it was designed for greater range and hitting power, TOW was mounted primarily on vehicles and, particularly, on attack helicopters. Helicopter-fired antitank missiles were first used in combat when the U.S. Army deployed several TOW-equipped UH-1 "Hueys" to Vietnam in response to the 1972 communist Easter offensive. TOW was the principal U.S. antiarmour munition until Hellfire, a more sophisticated helicopter-fired missile with semiactive laser and passive infrared homing, was mounted on the Hughes AH-64 Apache attack helicopter in the 1980s.

The British Swingfire and the French-designed, internationally marketed MILAN (*missile d'infanterie léger antichar*, or "light infantry antitank missile") and HOT (*haut subsonique optiquement téléguidé tiré d'un tube*, or "high-subsonic, optically teleguided, tube-fired") were similar in concept and capability to TOW.

The Soviets developed an entire family of antitank guided missiles beginning with the AT-1 Snapper, the AT-2 Swatter, and the AT-3 Sagger. (The AT designation and accompanying name were given by NATO to the Soviet missile systems. In this chapter, missile systems and aircraft of the former Soviet Union are referred to by their NATO designations.) The Sagger, a relatively small missile designed for infantry use on the lines of the original German concept, saw use in Vietnam and was used with conspicuous success by Egyptian infantry in the Suez Canal crossing of the 1973 Arab-Israeli War. The AT-6 Spiral, a Soviet version of TOW and Hellfire, became the principal antiarmour munition of Soviet attack helicopters.

Many antitank missile systems of later generations transmitted guidance commands by radio rather than by wire, and semiactive laser designation and passive infrared homing also became common. Guidance and control methods were more sophisticated than the original visual tracking and manual commands. TOW, for example, required the gunner simply to centre the reticle of his optical sight on the target, and the missile was tracked and guided automatically. Extremely thin optical fibres began to replace wires as a guidance link in the 1980s.

AIR-TO-SURFACE

The United States began to deploy tactical air-to-surface guided missiles as a standard aerial munition in the late

1950s. The first of these was the AGM-12 (for aerial guided munition) Bullpup, a rocket-powered weapon that employed visual tracking and radio-transmitted command guidance. The pilot controlled the missile by means of a small side-mounted joystick and guided it toward the target by observing a small flare in its tail. Though Bullpup was simple and accurate, the delivery aircraft had to continue flying toward the target until the weapon struck—a vulnerable maneuver. The 115-kg (250-pound) warhead on the initial version of Bullpup proved inadequate for "hard" targets such as reinforced concrete bridges in Vietnam, and later versions had a 450-kg (1,000-pound) warhead. The rocket-powered AGM-45 Shrike antiradiation missile was used in Vietnam to attack enemy radar and surface-to-air sites by passively homing onto their radar emissions. The first missile of its kind used in combat, the Shrike had to be tuned to the desired radar frequency before flight. Because it had no memory circuits and required continuous emissions for homing, it could be defeated by simply turning off the target radar. Following the Shrike was the AGM-78 Standard ARM (antiradiation munition), a larger and more expensive weapon that incorporated memory circuits and could be tuned to any of several frequencies in flight. Also rocket-propelled, it had a range of about 55 km (35 miles). Faster and more sophisticated still was the AGM-88 HARM (high-speed antiradiation missile), introduced into service in 1983.

Replacing the Bullpup as an optically tracked missile was the AGM-64/65 Maverick family of rocket-powered missiles. Early versions used television tracking, while later versions employed infrared, permitting the fixing of targets at longer ranges and at night. The self-contained guidance system incorporated computer logic that enabled the missile to lock onto an image of the target once the operator had identified it on his cockpit television monitor. Warheads varied from a 55-kg (125-pound) shaped charge for use against armour to high-explosive blast charges of 135 kg (300 pounds).

Though less was known about them, the Soviets fielded an extensive array of air-to-surface missiles equivalent to the Bullpup and Maverick and to the Hellfire antitank missile. Notable among these was the radio-command-guided AS-7 Kerry, the antiradar AS-8 and AS-9, and the television-guided AS-10 Karen and AS-14 Kedge (the last with a range of about 40 km, or 25 miles). These missiles were fired from tactical fighters such as the MiG-27 Flogger and attack helicopters such as the Mi-24 Hind and Mi-28 Havoc.

SURFACE-TO-AIR

Guided surface-to-air missiles, or SAMs, were under development when World War II ended, notably by the Germans, but were not sufficiently perfected to be used in combat. This changed in the 1950s and '60s with the rapid development of sophisticated SAM systems in the Soviet

Union, the United States, Great Britain, and France. With other industrialized nations following suit, surface-to-air missiles of indigenous design, particularly in the smaller categories, were fielded by many armies and navies.

The Soviet Union committed more technical and fiscal resources to the development of guided-missile air-defense systems than any other nation. Beginning with the SA-1 Guild, developed in the immediate postwar period, the Soviets steadily fielded SAMs of growing sophistication. These fell into two categories: systems such as the Guild, the SA-3 Goa, the SA-5 Gammon, and the SA-10 Grumble, which were deployed in defense of fixed installations; and mobile tactical systems capable of accompanying land forces. The SA-2 Guideline, introduced in 1958, was the most widely deployed of the early SAMs and was the first surface-to-air guided-missile system used in combat. This two-stage missile with a solid booster and a liquid-propellant (kerosene and nitric acid) sustainer, could engage targets at ranges of 45 km (28 miles) and as high as 18,000 metres (60,000 feet). Equipped with an array of van-mounted radars for target acquisition and tracking and for missile tracking and command guidance, Guideline proved effective in Vietnam. With adequate warning, U.S. fighters could outmaneuver the relatively large missiles, called "flying telephone poles" by pilots, and electronic countermeasures (ECM) reduced the effectiveness of the tracking radars; but,

while these SAMs inflicted relatively few losses, they forced U.S. aircraft down to low altitudes, where antiaircraft artillery and small arms exacted a heavy toll. Later versions of the SA-2 were equipped with optical tracking to counter the effects of ECM; this became a standard feature on SAM systems. After retirement from first-line Soviet service, the SA-2 remained in use in the Third World.

The SA-3 Goa, derived from the Guideline but modified for use against low-altitude targets, was first deployed in 1963—primarily in defense of fixed installations. The SA-N-1 was a similar naval missile.

The SA-4 Ganef was a long-range mobile system first deployed in the mid-1960s; the missiles, carried in pairs on a tracked launcher, used drop-off solid-fuel boosters and a ramjet sustainer motor. Employing a combination of radar command guidance and active radar homing, and supported by an array of mobile radars for target acquisition, tracking, and guidance, they could engage targets over the horizon. (Because the SA-4 strongly resembled the earlier British Bloodhound, NATO assigned it the code name Ganef, meaning "Thief" in Hebrew.) Beginning in the late 1980s, the SA-4 was replaced by the SA-12 Gladiator, a more compact and capable system.

The SA-6 Gainful was a mobile tactical system with a range of 3 to 55 km (2 to 35 miles) and a ceiling of 15,000 metres (50,000 feet). Three 6-metre (19-foot) missiles were carried

The Soviet SA-6 Gainful mobile surface-to-air missile system, developed during the 1960s, on maneuvers with armoured personnel carriers and truck-mounted artillery rockets.
Tass from Sovfoto

in canisters atop a tracked transporter-erector-launcher, or TEL, and the radar and fire-control systems were mounted on a similar vehicle, each of which supported four TELs. The missiles used semiactive radar homing and were powered by a combination of solid-rocket and ramjet propulsion. Gainful, the first truly mobile land-based SAM system, was first used in combat during the 1973 Arab-Israeli War and was highly effective at first against Israeli fighters.

The Mach-3 missile proved virtually impossible to outmaneuver, forcing the fighters to descend below effective radar coverage, where antiaircraft guns such as the ZSU 23-4 mobile system were particularly lethal. (Similar factors prevailed in the 1982 Falklands conflict, where long-range British Sea Dart missiles achieved relatively few kills but forced Argentine aircraft down to wave-top level.) Beginning in the 1980s, the SA-6 was replaced by the SA-11 Gadfly, a Mach-3 semiactive radar homing system with a range of 27 km (17 miles).

The SA-8 Gecko, first deployed in the mid-1970s, was a fully mobile system mounted on a novel six-wheeled amphibious vehicle. Each vehicle carried four canister-launched, semiactive radar homing missiles, with a range of about 7.5 miles, plus guidance and tracking equipment in a rotating turret. It had excellent performance but, in Syrian hands during the 1982 conflict in Lebanon, proved vulnerable to Israeli electronic countermeasures.

The SA-7 Grail shoulder-fired, infrared-homing missile was first deployed outside the Soviet Union in the final stages of the Vietnam War; it also saw extensive action in the Middle East. The SA-9 Gaskin carried four infrared-homing missiles on a turreted mount atop a four-wheeled vehicle. Its missiles were larger than the SA-7 and had more sophisticated seeker and guidance systems.

For 20 years, the most important land-based American SAM was the Hawk, a sophisticated system employing semiactive radar guidance. From the mid-1960s the Hawk provided the backbone of U.S. surface-based air defenses in Europe and South Korea and was exported to many allies. In Israeli use, Hawk missiles proved highly effective against low-flying aircraft. The longer-ranged Patriot missile system began entering service in 1985 as a partial replacement for the Hawk. Like the Hawk, the Patriot was semimobile; that is, the system components were not mounted permanently on vehicles and so had to be removed from their transport for firing. For target acquisition and identification, as well as for tracking and guidance, the Patriot system used a single phased-array radar, which controlled the direction of the beam by electronically varying the signals at several antennas rather than pivoting a single large antenna. The single-stage, solid-fueled Patriot missile was controlled by command guidance and employed track-via-missile homing, in which information from the radar in the missile itself was used by the launch site fire-control system.

The shoulder-fired Redeye, an infrared-homing missile that was also deployed on truck-mounted launchers, was fielded in the 1960s to provide U.S. Army units close-in protection against air attack. After 1980 the Redeye was replaced by the Stinger, a lighter system whose missile accelerated faster and whose more advanced seeker head could detect the hot exhaust of approaching aircraft even four miles away and up to 5,000 feet (1,500 metres) in altitude.

Western European mobile SAM systems include the German-designed Roland, an SA-8 equivalent fired from a variety of tracked and wheeled vehicles, and the French Crotale, an SA-6 equivalent that used a combination of radar command guidance and infrared terminal homing. Both systems were widely exported. Less directly comparable to Soviet systems was the British Rapier, a short-range, semimobile system intended primarily for airfield defense. The Rapier missile was fired from a small, rotating launcher that was transported by trailer. In the initial version, deployed in the early 1970s and used with some success in 1982 in the Falklands conflict, the target aircraft was tracked by a gunner using an optical sight. A television camera in the tracker measured differences between the missile's flight path and the path to the target, and microwave radio signals issued guidance corrections. The Rapier had a combat range of one-quarter to four miles (400 metres to 6.4 km) and a ceiling of 10,000 feet (3,000 metres). Later versions used radar tracking and guidance for all-weather engagements.

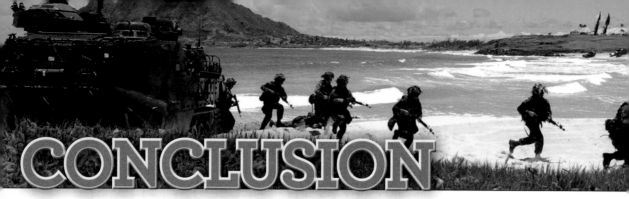

CONCLUSION

From the earliest times, a critical relationship has existed between military technology, the tactics of its employment, and the psychological factors that bind its users into units. Success in combat, the *sine qua non* of military organizations and the ultimate purpose of military technology, depends on the ability of the combatant group to coordinate the actions of its members in a tactically effective manner. This coordination is a function of the strength of the forces that bind the unit together, inducing its members to set aside their individual interests—even life itself—for the welfare of the group. These forces, in turn, are directly affected by both tactics and technology.

The influence of technology can be either positive or negative. The experience of the ancient Greek hoplite infantrymen is one example of positive influence. Their arms and armour were most effective for fighting in close formation. This type of battle led, in turn, to marching in step, which further augmented cohesion and made the phalanx a tactically formidable formation. The late medieval knight, however, offers an example of the negative influence of technology. To wield his sword and lance effectively, he and his charger needed considerable space, yet his closed helmet made communication with his fellows extremely difficult. It is not surprising, then, that knights of the late Middle Ages tended to fight as individuals, and were often defeated by cohesive units of less well-equipped opponents.

The interaction of tactics and technology—indeed, even the tension between the two—is even more important today, in an era when all of life seems to be dominated by technology. Yet even modern technologies cannot erase the fact that war on land is fundamentally a grim combat between determined people whose lives are firmly planted on the ground. This elemental nature of war on land will continue to be a force that shapes and even dominates technological change in the future.

ballista An ancient military engine often in the form of a crossbow for hurling large missiles.

breech The part of a firearm at the rear of the barrel.

calibre The diameter of a bore of a gun usually expressed in millimetres or hundredths or thousandths of an inch, and typically written as a decimal fraction.

catapult An ancient military device for hurling missiles.

crenellated Having open spaces used for defense or decoration.

cuirass A piece of armour covering the body from neck to waist.

culverin A firearm that was originally a rude musket but was in the 16th and 17th centuries a long cannon (as an 18-pounder) with serpent-shaped handles.

cupola A small structure built on top of a roof to provide interior lighting, to serve as a lookout, or for ornamental purposes.

drayage The act of hauling material on a cart or wagon without built-up sides.

frizzen The pivoted metal upright of the action of a flintlock against which the flint strikes upon firing.

gambeson A medieval garment of stuffed and quilted cloth or leather originally worn under the hauberk as a pad but later used alone as a defensive garment.

halberd A weapon especially of the 15th and 16th centuries consisting typically of a battle-axe and pike mounted on a handle about six feet long.

harquebus A matchlock gun invented in the 15th century which was portable but heavy and was usually fired from a support.

hauberk A tunic of chain mail worn as defensive armour from the 12th to the 14th century.

machicolation An opening in a parapet, floor, or roof through which missiles are discharged at assailants.

mandrel A metal bar that serves as a core around which material (as metal) may be cast, molded, forged, bent, or otherwise shaped.

mantelet A movable shelter formerly used by besiegers as a protection when attacking.

palisade A fence of stakes especially for defense.

phalanx A body of heavily armed infantry of ancient Greece.

portcullis A grating of iron hung over the gateway of a fortified place and lowered between grooves to prevent passage.

rampart A broad embankment raised as a fortification and usually surmounted by a parapet.

ravelin A detached work formerly used in fortifications and consisting of two embankments forming a salient angle in front of a fortified position.

recoil The kickback of a gun upon firing.

trebuchet A medieval military engine for hurling heavy missiles.

trunnion A pin or pivot on which something can be rotated or tilted; especially a cannon.

windlass Any of various machines for hoisting or hauling.

PREHISTORIC AND EARLY WARFARE

Arther Ferrill, *The Origins of War: From the Stone Age to Alexander the Great*, rev. ed. (1997), offers a scholarly survey of evidence for prehistoric war. Tim Everson, *Warfare in Ancient Greece: Arms and Armour from the Heroes of Homer to Alexander the Great* (2004), drawing on archaeological evidence and classical writings, discusses the weapons and tactics in use from about 1550 to 150 BCE. John Gibson Warry, *Warfare in the Classical World: An Illustrated Encyclopedia of Weapons, Warriors, and Warfare in the Ancient Civilisations of Greece and Rome* (1980, reissued 1995), is illustrated with photos, diagrams, maps, and battle plans. Victor Davis Hanson, *The Western Way of War: Infantry Battle in Classical Greece*, 2nd ed. (2009), by a prominent American historian, considers the links between culture, politics, and warfare. M.C. Bishop and J.C.N. Coulston, *Roman Military Equipment: From the Punic Wars to the Fall of Rome*, 2nd ed. (2006), is a well-illustrated book on changing technology. Adrian Keith Goldsworthy, *The Roman Army at War 100 BC–AD 200* (1996, reprinted 2009), part of the Oxford Classical Monographs series, surveys the organizing of war in the Roman era. Konstantin Nossov, *Ancient and Medieval Siege Weapons: A Fully Illustrated Guide to Siege Weapons and Tactics* (2005), is a well-illustrated popular history of siege-craft and siege weapons.

Brief historical surveys of equipment and dress, based on artistic interpretations of archaeological evidence, are presented in the works from the "Men-at-Arms" series: Terence Wise, *Ancient Armies of the Middle East* (1981), and *Armies of the Carthaginian Wars, 265–146 BC* (1982); Nick Sekunda, *The Ancient Greeks: Armies of Classical Greece, 5th and 4th Centuries BC* (1986), and *The Army of Alexander the Great* (1984); and Michael Simkins, *The Roman Army From Caesar to Trajan*, rev. ed. (1984).

WAR IN THE MIDDLE AGES

Maurice Keen (ed.), *Medieval Warfare: A History* (1999), is a collection of scholarly essays on topics from the age of the Vikings to the arrival of gunpowder. Nicholas Hooper and Matthew Bennett, *Cambridge Illustrated Atlas: Warfare: The Middle Ages 768–1487* (1996), combines maps, colour illustrations, and text to provide an informed yet popular survey of European warfare from the 8th through the 15th centuries. Paddy Griffith, *The Viking Art of War* (1995), by a historian and lecturer at Britain's Royal Military Academy at Sandhurst, analyzes the fighting organization and tactics of the Norse invaders.

David Nicolle, *Medieval Siege Weapons (1): Western Europe AD 585–1385* (2002), and *Medieval Siege Weapons (2): Byzantium, the Islamic World & India AD 476–1526* (2003), are two well-illustrated tours of siegecraft from western Europe to South Asia. J.E. Kaufmann and H.W. Kaufmann, *The Medieval Fortress: Castles, Forts, and Walled Cities of the Middle Ages* (2001), is an illustrated description of medieval European castles from a military perspective.

Ralph Payne-Gallwey, *The Crossbow, Mediaeval and Modern, Military and Sporting: Its Construction, History & Management, with a Treatise on the Balista and Catapult of the Ancients, and an Appendix on the Catapult, Balista & the Turkish Bow*, 2nd ed. (1958, reprinted 1981), remains the basic text on the crossbow; Robert Hardy, *Longbow: A Social and Military History* (1976, reissued 1986), is a definitive treatment by a famous archer, with appendixes on design and ballistics by technical experts.

The above-mentioned "Men-at-Arms" series includes Douglas Miller, *The Landsknechts* (1976) and *The Swiss at War, 1300–1500* (1979); David Nicolle, *Armies of the Ottoman Turks, 1300–1774* (1983); and S.R. Turnbull, *Samurai Armies, 1550–1615* (1979).

A.V.B. Norman, *The Medieval Soldier* (1971, reprinted 1993); and A.V.B. Norman and Don Pottinger, *English Weapons & Warfare, 449–1660* (1979, reissued 1985), are highly regarded older books that address weaponry in detail. Charles Ffoulkes,

Armour & Weapons (1909, reprinted 1973), remains a classic treatment of the development of personal armour in Europe.

THE GUNPOWDER REVOLUTION

Two books by academic historians, Bert S. Hall, *Weapons and Warfare in Renaissance Europe: Gunpowder, Technology, and Tactics* (1997); and Thomas Arnold, *The Renaissance at War* (2001), look closely at how warfare was changed as Europeans grew to understand the power of gunpowder weapons. Geoffrey Parker, *The Military Revolution: Military Innovation and the Rise of the West, 1500–1800*, 2nd ed. (1996), analyzes the impact of gunpowder on warfare and politics on a global scale. David Ayalon, *Gunpowder and Firearms in the Mamluk Kingdom: A Challenge to a Mediaeval Society*, 2nd ed. (1978), studies a military elite that failed to adapt to gunpowder.

For the transition to modern warfare, see William H. McNeill, *The Pursuit of Power: Technology, Armed Force, and Society Since A.D.1000* (1982), a broad overview of the political and economic effect of developments in military technology; Hew Strachan, *European Armies and the Conduct of War* (1983, reprinted 1991), which summarizes developments from the age of Frederick the Great onward; and Martin Van Creveld, *Technology and War: From 2000 B.C. to the Present*, rev. ed. (1991).

FORTIFICATION AND MODERN BODY ARMOUR

Christopher Duffy, *Fire and Stone: The Science of Fortress Warfare, 1660–1860* (1975, reprinted 2006), and *Siege Warfare* (vol. 1: *The Fortress in the Early Modern World, 1494–1660*, and vol. 2: *The Fortress in the Age of Vauban and Frederick the Great, 1680–1789*) (1979–85), treat the development of methods of siege craft and fortification and survey positional warfare.

J.E. Kaufmann and Robert M. Jurga, *Fortress Europe: European Fortifications of World War II* (1999), is an illustrated description of the Maginot Line, the Atlantic Wall, and other fortifications constructed throughout Europe before and during the war. John Ellis, *Eye-Deep in Hell: Trench Warfare in World War I* (1976, reissued 1989), is a graphic description of the misery of trench warfare. Stephen Bull, *Trench: A History of Trench Warfare on the Western Front* (2010), is a popular history.

Simon Dunstan and Ronald Volstad, *Flak Jackets: 20th Century Military Body Armour* (1984), in the "Men at Arms" series, surveys body armour from the helmets of the world wars to the flak jackets of Korea and Vietnam. Two books by Martin J. Brayley, *Tin Hats to Composite Helmets: A Collector's Guide* (2008), and *Modern Body Armour* (2011), provide a popular guide to the evolution of modern body armour in the 20th and 21st centuries.

SMALL ARMS AND ARTILLERY

A standard reference work by well-known firearms authorities offering encyclopaedic treatment is Ian V. Hogg and John S. Weeks, *Military Small Arms of the 20th Century*, 7th ed. (2000).

A classic reference work on small-arms development is Claude Blair (ed.), *Pollard's History of Firearms* (1983), a thorough reworking and modernizing of a 1927 book by British weaponry historian Hugh B.C. Pollard.

Histories of early small-arms development in various countries include Howard L. Blackmore, *British Military Firearms, 1650–1850* (1961); M.L. Brown, *Firearms in Colonial America: The Impact on History and Technology, 1492–1792* (1980); and John Walter, *The German Rifle: A Comprehensive Illustrated History of the Standard Bolt-Action Designs, 1871–1945* (1979).

Edward C. Ezell, *The AK-47 Story: Evolution of the Kalashnikov Weapons* (1986), focuses on Mikhail Kalashnikov's assault rifle but also includes a history of shoulder-weapons development in Russia and the Soviet Union from 1800 to the 1980s. Edward C. Ezell, *The Great Rifle Controversy: Search for the Ultimate Infantry Weapon from World War II Through Vietnam and Beyond* (1984), focuses on U.S. and NATO small-arms development, particularly the transition to assault rifles. Merritt Roe Smith, *Harpers Ferry Armory and the New*

Technology: The Challenge of Change (1977), discusses the American system of manufacture in its human and technological contexts. John Ellis, *The Social History of the Machine Gun* (1975, reprinted 1986), is an essay on the social impact of the machine gun.

Bruce I. Gudmundsson, *On Artillery* (1993), is a history of field artillery from the Franco-Prussian War of 1870–71 to the late 20th century. Ian V. Hogg, *A History of Artillery* (1974), though older, is a profusely illustrated history providing considerable technical detail on the development of arms from the 12th century to the 20th century. *Jane's Armour and Artillery* (annual) lists all current artillery weapons, with descriptions, specifications, and illustrations.

TANKS AND ARMOURED VEHICLES

The tanks and armoured vehicles of both world wars are described in detail in Richard M. Ogorkiewicz, *Armour: A History of Mechanized Forces* (1960, reissued as *Armoured Forces: A History of Armoured Forces and Their Vehicles*, 1970). The histories of various types of vehicles from World War I to the end of World War II are presented in books by Duncan Crow (ed.), such as *AFVs of World War One* (1970), *British AFVs, 1919–40* (1970), *British and Commonwealth AFVs, 1940–46* (1971), *American AFVs of World War II* (1972), and *Armored Fighting Vehicles of Germany: World War II* (1973). A useful reference source for German tanks, armoured vehicles, and self-propelled guns is Peter Chamberlain and Hilary L. Doyle. *Encyclopedia of German Tanks of World War Two*, rev. ed. (1993).

Illustrated histories of Soviet/Russian armour are provided in Wolfgang Fleischer, *Russian Tanks and Armored Fighting Vehicles, 1917–1945* (1999); Fred Koch, *Russian Tanks and Armored Vehicles, 1946 to the Present* (1999); and Andrew W. Hull, David R. Markov, and Steven J. Zaloga, *Soviet/Russian Armor and Artillery Design Practices: 1945 to Present* (1999). Popular histories of U.S. armour are offered in books by R.P. Hunnicut, including *Sherman: A History of the American Medium Tank* (1978), *Abrams: A History of the American Main Battle Tank* (1990), and *Bradley: A History of American Fighting and Support Vehicles* (1999). *Jane's Armour and Artillery* (annual) describes all current tanks.

ROCKET AND MISSILE SYSTEMS

The early years of military rockets are covered in Frank H. Winter, *The First Golden Age Of Rocketry: Congreve and Hale Rockets of the Nineteenth Century* (1990). Individual weapon systems are described in John Norris (ed.), *Anti-Tank Weapons* (1996), a volume in the "Brassey's Modern Military Equipment" series.

A

Alexander the Great, 6, 8, 13
amphibious assault vehicles, 136–137
antiaircraft and aerial rockets in WWII,
    152–153
antiaircraft artillery, 113, 115–118, 152–153
antitank weapons/guns, 100–101, 118, 129,
    150, 155–156
armour, body, 10–12
    bronze, 10
    mail, 10–11, 25–26
    modern, 55–56, 65–70
    plate, 12, 26–27
    types of, 11
armoured personnel carriers, 134–136
    fully tracked carriers, 135–136
    half-tracked carriers, 134–135
armoured vehicles, 134–142
arms, small
    the first, 52
    modern, 71–90
Armstrong, William, 103–104, 106
arrows, 16
artillery
    development of, 45–49
    early use of, 50–54
    modern, 102–119
assault rifle, 85–87
automatic weapons, 82–85
    self-loading rifle, 82–83
    submachine gun, 83–85
Avars, as horse archers, 33
ax, 9, 12

B

ballistics, refinements in, 44–45
Big Bertha, 62, 108, 109

body armour, modern, 55–56, 65–70
    new materials, 67–68
bow, 14, 15–17
    composite recurved, 2, 16–17, 33, 34
    crossbow, 35–38
    early, 16
    English longbow, 35, 36, 38
breechloaders, 77–82, 103–106
    bolt action, 78–79
    magazine repeaters, 81–82
    smokeless-powder revolution, 79–81
    wrought-iron, 46–48
Byzantine cataphract, 33–34

C

cannons, 49, 50–51, 102–115
    ammunition, 112–115
    carriages and mountings, 107–110
    cast-iron, 49
    fire control, 110–112
    recoil control, 106–107
    rifled bores, 103–106
castles, 29–31
    motte-and-bailey, 29–30
    stone fortifications, 30–31
cavalry
    age of, 22–28, 33
    shock cavalry of 4th century, 7–8
chariots, 20–21
China, military ecosphere of, 2, 33
Civil War, American, 59, 60, 61, 77, 78, 89, 147
classical age and antiquity, warfare in, 5–21
    defensive weaponry, 8–12
    fortification, 18–19
    land transportation, 19–21
    mechanical artillery, 17–18
    military technology, 7–8
    offensive weaponry, 12–17

coast guns, 107–108
Colt, Samuel, 88, 89, 90
Congreve, William, 145–147
crossbow, 35–38
Crusades, 23, 25, 26, 28, 35

E

elephants, 20
English longbow, 38
Eurasian Steppe, military ecosphere of,
2, 8, 33
Europe, military ecosphere of, 2, 8, 33

F

feudalism, 22, 25
field artillery, 108–110
flintlock, 53–54, 72, 74, 88, 91
fortification, 55, 56–65
bastioned trace, 59
classical age and antiquity, 18–19
duration of early modern, 59
effect of artillery and siegecraft on, 56–57
German channel defenses, 63–64
Maginot Line and West Wall, 62–63
Middle Ages, 29–31
nuclear, 64–65
permanent during WWI, 62
sunken profile, 57–58
and trench warfare, 60–61

G

Gatling, Richard J., 91, 92
Gatling gun, 91–92
Greek fire, 32–33
Greeks, and ancient warfare, 6, 9, 10, 11, 13, 15,
17, 18, 20
grenade launchers, 97–100
automatic fire, 98–100
single shot, 97–98
guncotton, 80
gunnery, 52

gunpowder revolution, 2, 40–54
corned powder, 42–44
development of artillery, 45–49
early gunpowder, 42–45
early use of artillery, 50–54
recipes for, 43
refinements in ballistics, 44–45
serpentine powder, 42

H

halberd, 39
helmets, 9, 26, 27
horse archer, 2, 8, 33–35
Byzantine cataphract, 33–34
Huns and Avars, 33
Mongols, 34–35
Turks, 34
horses, 2, 8, 19–21, 108
age of cavalry, 22–28, 33
war-horse, 20, 27–28
Huns, as horse archers, 33

I

infantry fighting vehicles, 137–139
infantry revolution, 35–39
Iraq War, 68, 136, 137, 142

J

javelin, 13, 14
Jericho, walls of, 2

K

Kevlar, 67, 68
Key, Francis Scott, 146
knight, the medieval, 23–25
mail armour, 25–26
orders of, 23–25
plate armour, 26–27
Korean War, 67, 87, 135, 136, 150
Krupp, Alfred, 103–104, 105, 106

L

legion, 7

M

mace/mace head, 2–4, 9
machine guns and specialty shoulder weapons, 91–101
 antitank weapons, 100–101
 and blowback, 94–95
 early manual multibarreled weapons, 91–93
 gas operation, 94
 grenade launchers, 97–100
 heavy machine guns, 93–95
 large-calibre machine guns, 96–97
 light machine guns, 95–96
 and recoil, 93–94
 submachine gun, 83–85
Maginot Line, 62–63
maniples, 6–7
matchlock, 52–53, 72
Maxim, Hiram, 82, 89, 93
Middle Ages, war in the, 22–39
 and cavalry, 22–31
 and the horse archer, 33–35
 the infantry revolution, 35–39
 siege weapons, 31–33
military ecospheres, 1–2
Minié, Claude-Étienne, 76
Minié rifles, 76–77
missiles, tactical guided, 143, 153–161
 guidance methods, 153–155
 guided-missile systems, 155–161
mitrailleuse, 92–93
Mongols, as horse archers, 34–35
mortars, 115
muzzle-loaders, 88, 105
 cast bronze, 48–49
 rifled, 75–77
 smoothbore, 72–75
 wrought-iron, 45–46

N

nuclear fortification, 64–65

P

Petersburg, Va., siege of, 61
phalanx, 5–6
Philip II of Macedon, 6, 8
pike, 39
pistols, 88–90
 revolvers, 88–89
 self-loaders, 89–90
prehistoric and early warfare, 1–21

R

recoilless guns, 119
rockets, 143–153
 antiaircraft and aerial in WWII, 152–153
 barrage, 149–150
 bazookas and Panzerschrecks, 150–152
 Congreve, 144–147
 rocketry research and experimentation, 147–148
Romans, and ancient warfare, 6–7, 10, 11, 12, 13, 15, 17–19

S

Sherman tank, 126
shields, 9–10
shot, special-purpose, 51–52
shoulder weapons, 71–87
 specialty, 97–101
siege weapons, 31–33, 56–57
sling, 13–14
small arms
 the first, 52
 modern, 71–90
spear, 12–13
"Star Spangled Banner, The," 146
sword, 14–15

T

tanks, 120–134
  antitank guns/weapons, 100–101, 118, 129, 150, 155–156
  armament, 129–132
  armour, 132–133
  configuration, 134
  earliest developments, 120–121
  interwar developments, 123–125
  mobility, 133–134
  postwar tank development, 128–134
  in WWI, 121–123
  in WWII, 125–128
trebuchet, 31–32
trench warfare (1850–1918), 60–61, 66
Turks, as horse archers, 34

V

Vietnam War, 67, 87, 97, 98, 101, 135, 155, 157, 158

W

war-horse, 27–28
weapons
  in antiquity and the classical age, 5, 8–17
  earliest military, 2–4
  and gunpowder revolution, 40–54
  machine guns and specialty shoulder weapons, 91–101
  in Middle Ages, 35–39
  modern artillery, 102–119
  modern small arms, 71–90
  precious metals to base metals, 4
  siege, 31–33
West Wall (WWII), 63–64
wheeled armoured vehicles, 139–142
wheel lock, 53, 72, 88
World War I
  permanent fortification during, 62
  tanks in, 100, 121–123
  trench warfare, 60–61
  weapons in, 81, 82, 83, 85, 94, 95, 97, 100, 108, 109, 111, 113, 116, 148
World War II
  antiaircraft and aerial rockets in, 152–153
  armoured vehicles in, 134–135, 136, 137
  fort series in, 63
  German channel defenses in, 63–64
  Maginot Line and West Wall, 62–63
  Sherman tank, 126
  tanks in, 100, 125–128
  weapons in, 83, 84, 85, 88, 95, 98, 100, 105, 113, 114–115, 116, 118, 148, 149, 150–151